The Zoot-Suit Riots

Mexican American Monograph Number 8
The Center for Mexican American Studies
The University of Texas at Austin

THE PSYCHOLOGY OF SYMBOLIC ANNIHILATION

The
Zoot-Suit
Riots
Mauricio Mazón

University of Texas Press, Austin

Eighth paperback printing, 2008

Requests for permission to reproduce material from this work
should be sent to:
  Permissions
  University of Texas Press
  P.O. Box 7819
  Austin, TX 78713-7819
  www.utexas.edu/utpress/about/bpermission.html

∞The paper used in this book meets the minimum requirements
of ANSI/NISO Z39.48-1992 (R1997) (Permanence of Paper).

Library of Congress Cataloging-in-Publication Data
Mazón, Mauricio, 1945–
  The zoot-suit riots.
  Bibliography: p.
  Includes index.
  1. Mexican Americans—California—Los Angeles—History.
  2. Mexican Americans—California—Los Angeles—Psychology.
  3. Los Angeles (Calif.)—Riot, 1943. I. Title.
F869.L89M56 1984 979.4'940046872 84-5656
ISBN 978-0-292-79803-8 pbk.

The Cartoons "'Zoot Suit' Yokum" are reprinted with permission
from *Li'l Abner: A Study in American Satire* by Arthur Asa Berger
(Boston: Twayne Publishers, Inc., 1970), pp. 77–88.
Photograph on the title page courtesy of the *Los Angeles Times*
© 1943 *Los Angeles Times*

In Memory of My Mother
María del Carmen Mazón

And to My Father
Valentín Mazón

Contents

Preface

If an hysterical patient went to a physician in the late nineteenth century, chances were the diagnostic focus would be on the somatic symptomatology. The patient exhibiting hysterical blindness or paralysis was treated by an ophthalmologist or neurologist, who looked for pathological evidence of disease, deterioration, or damage. These procedures signaled a triumph over an earlier view that perceived hysteria as a largely female complaint in which a woman's uterus detached itself and floated about throughout her body.[1] With the work of Charcot, Janet, and especially Freud, hysteria came to be appreciated as an anxiety reaction whose pathological locus was emotional, not physiological, and was therefore not restricted to women.

Today popular wisdom recognizes that certain cardiopulmonary, gastrointestinal, and neurological symptoms originate with severe psychological stress. Nevertheless, the attraction persists for accepting the manifest sign or symptom as the most accurate measure of mental and physical health. There is an obvious need to grapple with manifest behavior. But in some instances the more accurate interpretation of behavior is to be found in latent material. The word "hysteria" in ordinary usage denotes the loss of self-control and a diminished if not total incapacity for rational and logical thinking. Hysterical individuals therefore represent chaos, disorder, and a loss of reality testing. Yet the hysterical individual may also represent a complicated organization in which the overt symptoms of emotional collapse serve to conceal personality deficits and conflicts. Where the outward impression presented by the hysterical individual may seem disorderly, it may also signify a series of psychologically defensive maneuvers designed to maintain a distorted but nevertheless cohesive internal sense of order.

In history the crowd has often been likened to the hysterical individual. In his celebrated nineteenth-century study, Gustave Le Bon included the following in his convictions about crowd behavior: "It will be remarked that among the special characteristics of crowds there are several—such as impulsiveness, irritability, incapacity to reason, the absence of judgment and of the critical spirit, the exaggeration of the sentiments, and others besides—which are almost always observed in beings belonging to inferior forms of evolution—in women, savages, and children, for instance."[2] This view and its attendant derivatives held sway among otherwise critical minds in the nineteenth century and has strong adherents in the twentieth. Thus the crowd, frequently downgraded to the "mob," has been associated with the loss of rational faculties and the stimulation of atavistic tendencies. However, some historians have made concerted efforts to revise our understanding of crowds by identifying the various levels of political awareness that define crowd behavior. Eric Hobsbawn, George Rude, and Charles Tilly have led the way with their respective studies of European and American crowds, mass movements, and riots. About crowds in the eighteenth and nineteenth centuries, Rude makes this representative comment: "Yet, though riots tended to follow traditional patterns, even the most short lived of them rarely appeared entirely ready made. Even a local strike or food riot would gain momentum from smaller beginnings and have clearly defined points of departure, climax, and conclusion."[3] The analogy may be drawn between our contemporary appreciation of the hysterical personality and our appreciation of crowds, mobs, and riots. Both the individual and the group, even at their most persuasive levels of disorganization, are imbued with structural sophistication that allows for ideology or politics; in short, some levels of conscious premeditation. The direction is, therefore, toward acknowledging various degrees of consciousness and awareness that remove the stigma of irrationality, primitiveness, and political naiveté from the crowd.

Rude and his cohorts fully appreciated areas of crowd behavior that were not politically motivated: "Nevertheless, in general, we may exclude from our present considerations crowds that are casually drawn together, like sight-seers; crowds assembled on purely ceremonial occasions or crowds taking part in religious or academic processions; or 'audience' crowds (as they have been termed) who gather in theaters or lecture halls, at baseball matches or bullfights, or who used to witness hangings. . . ."[4] The issue remains—although for some, like anthropologists, the problem is worded differently—whether the preceding are indeed apolitical.[5] Somewhere between the boundaries of a Le Bon and a Rude are cumbersome areas that fit in neither category and that incorporate elements of both.

One of the best examples of the latter in American history is the Zoot-Suit Riots of 1943. The study of crowd behavior as interpreted by Hobsbawn, Rude, and Tilly argues for points of historical continuity and departure that are politically and ideologically delineated. An initial and cursory examination of the Zoot-Suit Riots falls well within these parameters. There was the standing precedent of discrimination against Mexicans in California in both the nineteenth and twentieth centuries. Political, racial, economic, educational, and even religious discrimination were de facto realities of 1943 Los Angeles. Yet there were some significant countercurrents.

Perhaps the most noticeable was the creation of the Bracero Program in 1942. This international accord between Mexico and the United States provided for the importation of thousands of Mexican farmworkers. The original purpose was to release American fieldhands for work in defense industries or military service. In some instances braceros ended up working in defense-related jobs, although it was specifically against the protocols of the agreement. Both sides agreed the Bracero Program was Mexico's single most important contribution to the war effort. Cooperation was also evident between the Mexican and American military services. Naval units from the two countries exchanged information about potential Japanese activities in Baja California, and the Mexican army was quick to rescue and return American pilots and their planes whenever they crash-landed in Mexican territory. At the time of the riot Mexican naval officers were in training in San Diego—an exercise intended to upgrade their surveillance capabilities and to foster better relations between the two countries. On 5 May 1943, Mexican soldiers paraded in downtown Los Angeles in celebration of the defeat of the French at Puebla. The epitome of this cooperative honeymoon was the organization of special social functions for the daughters of the Mexican and American admirals. These were powerful symbolic and political gestures of goodwill.

The political and psychological perception of Mexicans and Mexican Americans in the war years is a complicated matter. The advent of the Zoot-Suit Riots crystalized areas of ambiguity and introduced a new perception of Mexican Americans—the condensed imagery of gangs, pachucos, and zoot-suiters. It was easy for contemporaries on the political Left to see the riots as a recrudescence of the racism that flourished in the immediate and distant past. If there was a difference it seemed to be that a wider press coverage was given to the alleged antics of zoot-suiters, and that the targets of the combined efforts of servicemen, civilians, and law enforcement agencies was restricted to youth.

However, the extraordinary quality of the riots is found in the symbolic means through which servicemen attacked zoot-suiters. Instead of directly acting out their grievances and launching a maniacal reign of destruction, the attack on zoot-suiters remained largely an indirect expression of the unconscious angst of young recruits. The overwhelming predominance of symbolic behavior in a group poses a challenge to historians. Is historical meaning to be found in the manifest or latent content of human events?

This study emphasizes the analysis of symbolic expressions as they unfolded during the ten-day riots that revealed elements of the impulsive characteristics described by Le Bon and elements of consciously formulated—albeit often distorted—political agendas. It is important to make a disclaimer about the scope and limits undertaken in this work. This book makes no pretense about presenting a history of the Zoot-Suit Riots, Chicano youth, or the social status of Mexican Americans during the Second World War. Nor is it an attempt to present a chronology of the riots from their initial incident to the waning moments of the last confrontation. The focus, rather, is on the latent, unconscious, and irrational processes that describe and identify the underlying assumptions and distortions in the behavior of servicemen, the military command in general, the press, the local and state bureaucracies, and the investigatory activities of political committees and law enforcement agencies. In a manner similar to the diagnostic approach and treatment of the hysterical personality, the objective here is to ascertain the nature of the covert structures, continuities, and hierarchies that give the riots psychological and historical meaning. As such, this work is an alternative to studies that have understood the riots within a more literal, traditional, and manifest context. Common among the preceding is an approach that accentuates the centrality of racial conflict and socioeconomic deprivation in the formation of gangs. These studies offer invaluable insights into the social and political history of Mexican Americans in the war years; however, few if any have benefited from previously unavailable navy and army accounts that make it possible to broaden the interpretation of the riots beyond the confines of the barrio.

The bulk of the military records pertaining to the riots are found at the Federal Archives and Records Center in Laguna Niguel, California. Although the records are housed at this location, they remain under the authority of the commandant of the Eleventh Naval District in San Diego. The records are kept in three boxes with some of the more important materials found in files P8-5, EF-44, and P13-5. Together these files contain transcripts of conversations; telegrams; letters from military commanders, civilians, and politicians; arrest records; and both army and navy memos. These documents reveal a tale that is radically different from popular assumptions about the riots. Many of the documents are classified restricted and attest somewhat graphically to the importance given the riots by the military high command. The United States Navy promptly responded to my request to examine these files by granting unconditional permission, and the staff of the Laguna Niguel Federal Archives and Records Center generously facilitated the research by assisting in the location and photocopying of the necessary materials.

The National Chicano Council on Higher Education kindly awarded me a one-year, postdoctoral fellowship that made full-time work on the manuscript possible. The University of Southern California was equally supportive in presenting me with a Haynes Summer Grant.

Several colleagues have read all or part of the manuscript. Some listened to my evolving formulations and surely have heard more about the riots than is necessary in a lifetime. But without exception, I have derived a greater understanding of my work from all of them. It pleases me to acknowledge the advice and support of Rodolfo Acuña (who unselfishly shared Federal Bureau of Investigation records relating to the riots), Luis Arroyo, Peter Loewenberg, Frank Mitchell, D. Brendan Nagle, Edwin Perkins, Richard Rollins, and Renato Rosaldo, Jr. I am especially indebted to Scott Lubeck and Ricardo Romo.

The solitude of writing and rewriting was joyfully broken by Rosa Maria and Rafael with gifts of merriment and spontaneity. And as always, Janet lobbied against my rationalizations, moderated my excesses, and endlessly conspired to keep me acquainted with perspective.

Alhambra, California
6 February 1983

The Zoot-Suit Riots

1. Introduction

The Zoot-Suit Riots occurred in Los Angeles between 3 to 13 June 1943. They are a remarkable event in that they defy simple classification. They were not about zoot-suiters rioting, and they were not, in any conventional sense of the word, "riots." No one was killed. No one sustained massive injuries. Property damage was slight. No major or minor judicial decisions stemmed from the riots. There was no pattern to arrests. Convictions were few and highly discretionary. There were no political manifestos or heroes originating from the riots, although later on the riots would assume political significance for a different generation.

What the riots lack in hard incriminating evidence they make up for in a plethora of emotions, fantasies, and symbols. This is not unusual in crowd behavior or is it a recent development in American history. Peter Shaw in *American Patriots and the Rituals of Revolution* (1981) begins his book by noting the similarities between Colonial and contemporary riots:

> The Stamp Act riots of August 1765 shocked the English speaking world. Despite a history of far more violent crowd disturbances in the American colonies, these gatherings elicited special concern. Opponents of the Stamp Act expressed as much surprise and dismay as its supporters, and both sides took steps to prevent a repetition of the violence. Two hundred years later, in the 1960s, street disturbances in which a few people were injured could similarly elicit sharper reactions than acts of violence in which scores were killed. At both times the expressive behavior of crowds proved more important than their actual deeds. Repeatedly the rioters emphasized, and the authorities reacted to, this behavior rather than the situation objectively considered. To participants and observers alike, the ritual proved more important than the reality.[1]

The ritual, in the Zoot-Suit Riots, was likewise more important than the reality. The zoot-suiters, attacked by servicemen and civilians in June 1943, were symbolically annihilated, castrated, transformed, and otherwise rendered the subjects of effigial rites. Among the bizarre processes was the transformation of the real zoot-suiter into an imaginary zoot-suiter. This remarkable invention is externalized evidence of the internal mental activities of adults and youths in the American home front. These mental activities had specific functions, and it is through the interpretation of these functions that the multiple meanings of the Zoot-Suit Riots achieved historical importance.

Since the riots elude the usual categories of interpretation and explication, the initial problem is where to begin. An obvious approach is to give a chronology of the events leading to the riots. Yet because of the predominance of inverted forms of behavior, the symmetry of the riots is not to be found in either chronology or historical antecedent, although there obviously is a chronology and continuity with the past. One approach is to describe the significance of the zoot-suiter both as a real and imagined entity.

The Zoot-Suit Riots were ostensibly a confrontation between Anglo servicemen and Mexican-American zoot-suiters. The term was largely one of attribution, for Mexican-American youth preferred other descriptions. Long before the riots Mexican and Mexican Americans were the beneficiaries, victims, and often the authors of other descriptive terms. One of the more widely recognized is the term *cholo*—today's version of the 1940s pachuco. Leonard Pitt in the *Decline of the Californios* (1971) writes about bands of cholos who migrated to California in the 1830s and 1840s. He translated cholo to mean "scoundrel," then used it as a synonym for lower-class, uneducated, and recently arrived Mexicans.[2] Cholo also described the type of Mexican soldier sent to California in the 1840s, an army that counted a liberal contingent of felons in its ranks. The term endured as one of derision throughout the nineteenth and twentieth centuries. Aside from denoting Mexican immigrants to California, cholo signified a group of people who were economically and educationally oppressed. Small wonder then that another variant of cholo and pachuco, the *bato vago*, was associated with the poor who fought in the Mexican Revolution with Francisco Villa: "Antes de que fueran pachucos, antes de los tiempos míos, les decían batos vagos, me entiendes . . . y esos son los batos que pelearon en la Revolución con Pancho Villa [Before they were pachucos, before my time, they called them batos vagos, you know . . . and they were the batos who fought in the Revolution with Pancho Villa]."[3]

But perhaps the more persistent connection between the cholo of the nineteenth century and the pachuco of the twentieth is seen in a common linguistic tradition. Chicano scholars have at times identified

Calo as the privileged language of the Mexican-American barrio. And for many, Caló is a barrio creation largely credited to neologisms of Mexican-American youth. This version of regional pride is understandable, but historically incorrect. Caló was neither a pachuco nor a new world contribution. "Caló has its ancient roots buried deeply in the fertile gypsy tongue (Calé, Romano, Zincalé and Calogitano, which is a lingo of Calé); classic Castellano . . . fractured in spelling, crippled in meaning; mutilated French, English, Italian, and the dead languages of Latin, Greek, and Hebrew, plus medieval Moorish."[4] Caló, originally *zincaló*, was the idiom of Spanish gypsies—one of the many minorities in Spain. The conquistadores brought Caló to the New World. Already identified by the upper classes as the argot of the criminal, the poor, and the uneducated, Caló and its variants became well known to the conquered Indian. The indigenous masses of the New World augmented the peninsular Caló with their own modifications and inventions. Spanish, in its florid dialects, idioms, and argots, unified the New with the Old World. Linguists may well dwell on multiple derivatives of Spanish in both continents. There is *jerigonza*, the lingo of criminals. There is *jacarandana*, the lingo of prostitutes. And then there is a grouping: *calico, calichi, calomel, calorama, calorin, calostro*, all of which mean Caló. Along with the high culture of Spain, the New World inherited a style of communication that was politically, socially, and economically determined. The fruits of this inexorable process of cultural transmission were seen in the dissemination of Caló in Mexico and the United States:

> Transmitted horizontally through migrations from border towns, but particularly from the central plateau—the states of Jalisco, Michoacan and Mexico City—the dialect, northwardbound from the areas where it traditionally existed, found a setting in El Paso, historically a stepping stone into the Southwest, especially as the city turned into a clearing house for Mexican labor.[5]

Thus the pachuco youth of Los Angeles and the Southwest, however impoverished, were the heirs of a linguistic and therefore cultural tradition originating in fifteenth-century Spain. When the batos of East Los Angeles talked about *la julia*, they meant to evoke the dread of the paddy wagon shared by their continental predecessors. And when the batos talked about *calcos*, most were probably oblivious of the fact that gitanos used the same word for shoes.

Seldom was the pachuco introduced as the descendant of cholos, gypsies, and other figures from both the Old and New Worlds. The pachucos' use of Caló merely confirmed their deviance from proper Spanish, rather than placing them within a tradition that had survived half a millennium. By the 1940s the historical antecedents of the pachuco were of secondary importance. Even the sensitive Carey McWilliams showed impatience with the question of origins: "Many theories have been advanced and reams of paper wasted in an attempt to define the origin of the word 'pachuco.' "[6] He nevertheless offered a theory:

> Some say that the expression originally came from Mexico and denoted resemblance to the gaily costumed people living in a town (Pachuca) of this name; others have said that it was first applied to border bandits in the vicinity of El Paso. Regardless of the origin of the word, the pachuco stereotype was born in Los Angeles.[7]

The "birth" of the pachuco is linked to the movement of Mexicans from rural to urban centers, to a generational rebellion against both Mexican and American culture, to the influx of drugs, and to an enduring legacy of discrimination. The good intentions of McWilliams converted the pachuco into something of a spontaneous development, a kind of ahistorical being that could be further distorted by law enforcement authorities.

Several writers, like Beatrice Griffith, attempted to reduce the pachuco's negative image: "You find youth of Scotch-Irish Protestant, Jewish or Italian, Russian or Negro background who have learned to speak Spanish with Pachuco emphasis, wear the traditional Pachuco clothes and haircuts, and otherwise become lost in the group."[8] McWilliams, too, contributed to this effort in describing "Victor Rodman Thompson, twenty-one . . . an Anglo youngster who, by long association with the Mexican boys in his neighborhood, had become completely Mexicanized."[9] Griffith offers another vignette: "There is one blue-eyed Irish boy living in a Mexican community who has so completely adopted the pachuco culture pattern that he sings and creates corridos, the old Mexican folk ballads that the Pachucos make up for purposes of song and gang gossip."[10] The pachucos themselves often reflected the prejudices of the city: "In one instance a Mexican club leader refused to allow the boys to play football with either Negro or Anglo-American youth."[11]

The pachuco élan of the Mexican American extended well into Mexico. Carlos Monsivais, internationally known critic of Mexican and American cultures, dated the beginning of Mexico's fascination with pachucos with the debut in 1945 of Germán Valdés, popularly recognized as "Tin Tan." "His gimmick was the pachuco character-type developed in Los Angeles."[12] Ironically, Mexican audiences saw Tin Tan as a victim of Anglo-American assimilation: "the pachuco as embodied by Tin Tan and gigolo characters (*cinturitas*) in cabaret-style movies, was no more than a comic representation of a type intoxicated by the American way of life."[13] The pachuco insulted Mexican tastes:

> . . . the character of Tin Tan proved difficult to sponsor. Motion picture censorship, intent on preserving purity of custom and language, urged on even by language academicians, soon found fault with the pachuco, demanding that he tone down or change his speech, diminish his obvious cultural borrowing, and become just another urban comedian, free of what was precisely his significance.[14]

For many Mexicans the pachuco represented the crystallization of the *pocho*, i.e., a Mexican born in the United States; alien to both cultures; fluent in neither Spanish nor English; a specialist in Caló, the argot of lumpen elements—an ideal subject for ethnocentric apologies or chauvinistic attacks. In Mexico the pachuco was perceived as a caricature of the American, while in the United States the pachuco was proof of Mexican degeneracy.

Significantly, many gang members were just discovering the pachuco style in the early 1940s. Joan Moore and her collaborators underscored the disparity in the self-identity of various gangs in *Homeboys, Gangs, Drugs and Prison in the Barrios of Los Angeles* (1978). The Polviados from the Los Angeles suburb of San Fernando are an example:

> But the real model for the Polviados were the pachucos of Los Angeles. The gang started in the early 1940s, and made a point of keeping up with the latest clothing fads, going to Murray's and Young's in downtown Los Angeles for their drapes and fingertip coats, and to Price's for their double-soled shoes. The Polviados consciously set themselves apart from the rural Chicanos of Pacoima, Canoga Park, Van Nuys and other Valley barrios, whom they considered backward, square, "farmers."[15]

Theirs was a social hierarchy that highlighted coiffure, garb, and select membership. Other Mexican-American youth "sneered at the Polviados' 'anti-macho' effort to smell pretty and look dandy."[16] Some considered the zoot suit to be childish: "In the early 1940s, when the zoot-suit fad swept over the Chicano youth of Los Angeles, the young men of La Puríssima [White Fence] gang jeered it as a kid's fad.[17]" It is important to know that the White Fence gang was the "first Chicano gang in East Los Angeles to use serious weapons—

chains and, occasionally, guns.''[18] Thus the zoot-suit fad that had swept the United States and even Europe came late to the barrio of Los Angeles.

The most dramatic changes for American youth were hardly restricted to the barrios. Youth exploded on the home front after a decade of virtual anonymity. The Great Depression was the decade of adults who struggled for jobs in a depressed economy. The government eased the impact of young people coming into the job market by diverting them into the National Youth Administration (NYA) and the Civilian Conservation Corps (CCC). All of this changed with the beginning of the Second World War. By early 1942 cities bristled with young servicemen in uniform as they savored weekend liberty or commuted from one assignment to another. Trains and buses were filled with servicemen in transit. Countless civic and national organizations sprang to meet their lodging and boarding needs. The press, radio, and movie industries clamored for features on the travails, exploits, sorrows, and glories of young men and women in the armed forces. The convulsive presence of millions of young people being readied for war redefined the relationship between parents and children. The war distorted the maturation of adolescence. It confronted them prematurely with entering into permanent decisions when the war, by definition, stood for impermanence. It stretched their psyches in opposite directions. Those too young or exempted from military duty found lucrative employment in an economy geared for total war. Compared with the 1930s, money was plentiful and the promise of continued prosperity was unlimited. Still, the war nullified all hope for the thousands who died or were physically and mentally incapacitated. The brutal dichotomy between life and death and the intervening stresses were negotiated by a series of activities unique to wartime. When concerned citizens and custodians of morality sounded the alarm of increased vice, vandalism, and violence among youth, they failed to consider these predictable contraventions of social norms as reflections of the licensed contraventions of total war.

The ideal of American youth was encapsulated in the serviceman. The need for heroes was an obvious element in the psychological and physical regime for mobilizing the nation. But the hero flourished only in contradistinction to the antihero. As youth were subjected to the alerted scrutiny of the press, law enforcement agents, and elder adults, several categories became discernible. Among the more observable antiheroic youth groups were the zoot-suiters.

The zoot suit was an international phenomenon. "In London the Zoot-Suit was worn mainly by street traders known as 'spivs' or 'wide boys' who lurked at street corners to offer you nylons and other goods in short supply."[19] The origins of the zoot-suit? One knowledgeable guess was "that it had been invented by a Saville Row tailor named E. P. Scholte at the close of the nineteenth century, and Scholte had adapted it from Guards officers' greatcoats."[20] Another view was that Clark Gable, as Rhett Butler in *Gone with the Wind,* had popularized it. Some contended that it originated in Harlem among blacks. There were several derivatives. Among them was the "Edwardian look"—a favorite of "Teddy Boys" that featured "narrow 'drainpipe' trousers and jacket (with deep cuffs) buttoning high, sometimes worn with a fancy vest."[21] The zoot suit gained additional notoriety among fad-conscious adolescents when it was sported by national idols:

> The Drape Shape, as if made for a much larger man than its wearer, so baggy as to conceal a bad figure but with ample room for a holster under the armpit, was associated with American gangsters, and a version of it known as the Zoot-Suit had been worn by Danny Kaye and Frank Sinatra for a short time.[22]

The intrusion of the zoot-suiter into the conventions of adult society was met with anger, shock, and undoubtedly envy. The zoot-suiter was the antithesis of the serviceman and disrupted the roles assigned to adolescents. "Teenagers ," who represented another invention of the war years, were more independent economically than any preceding generation of American youth. They made their tastes directly felt in matters of clothing, movies, music, and language, and their younger siblings copied them.

Indeed, the quick affluence of full-time employment combined with the omnipresence of the war produced extremes in reality that were met by excesses in youthful behavior. "They bought new clothes, cars, records; went out more often; and pushed the marriage rate up by 20 percent."[23] What distinguished the young of the epoch had distinguished the generation before them: "A sizable number began to emphasize the distance between themselves and the rest of society by donning the most outlandish clothing since their parents were young—that is, since the fabled twenties."[24] Instead of the Charleston they danced the jitterbug, with music ideally suited to the loose-fitting Drape Shapes of the zoot-suiters. With their ankle-tight pegged cuffs, reet pleats, peg tops, lids, and DA hairstyles, the zoot-suiters flaunted their disdain for adult conventions with the garish insolence of rebellious youth. Like their parents during the 1920s, the younger generation of the early 1940s accompanied their adolescent iconoclasm with irreverent hit songs. Among the more popular were "I Wanna Zoot-Suit" and "A Zoot-Suit."[25]

In keeping with most fads the zoot suit was more conspicuous in large cities. New York City, Detroit, Chicago, Philadelphia, and Los Angeles were the trendsetters. Besides being the ideal attire for dancing the jitterbug the zoot suit also represented defiance. Fritz Redl, the noted child psychiatrist, warned in 1943 about "premature generalizations" concerning zoot-suiters.[26] He was not seeking publicity when he suggested that "the zoot suit cult had penetrated to some extent among middle class youth."[27] The very stylized and customized nature of the suit made it expensive, with the more flamboyant versions being financially out of reach for many lower-class youths. But whether chic or plain, the zoot suit was an evocative and provocative symbol. According to Redl, the zoot suit provided "youth with a *symbolic* anticipation of being adult. It may do so in many ways, and one is through emphasis on adult-hoarded pleasures and licenses, transgressions against adult *tabus* and supervision, rejection of adult values and behavior standards."[28]

Redl did not consider the generalized behavior of zoot-suiters as pathological. Nor did he consider them politically minded. He also warned about hasty efforts at correcting their behavior: "To attempt to satisfy zoot suiters by making them members of an organized Boy Scout troop would be as unsuccessful as trying to build them into a 'party' with definite goals or political or social programs."[29]

The pachuco and zoot-suiter thus confronted American society with an apparent historical discontinuity. Both represented an unprecedented development—or so at least it must have seemed to adults who with the benefit of a protective amnesia had forgotten the libertines and bohemians of the 1920s. The surface dissimilarities between the pachuco zoot-suiter, serviceman, and adult civilian restricted any relationship to an adverse level. Instead of structuring the relationship between, say, zoot-suiters and servicemen in the language of two categories of youth facing problems of maturation, rebellion, and identity confusion, the relationship was usually framed in the most antagonistic terms. This trend survived in the narratives on the riots as both liberal and conservative interpretations demonstrated the profound differences between the various factions.

The tendency to highlight the dissociative elements of the Zoot-Suit Riots is undoubtedly influenced by the obvious differences in the race, age, class, and even language of the participants. One can readily concede that it is the matter of irreconcilable differences that provokes violence at the individual, group, and national levels. However, for this study a more promising approach is to find the unifying themes that brought zoot-suiters, servicemen, and civilians together for the ten-day pseudoriots. Among the more significant pieces of information is the fact that neither the zoot-suiter nor the "riots" make sense.

The zoot-suiters projected a deceptively anarchistic image. Especially nonsensical to adults were aspects of their garb, gait, and argot. Redl himself had trouble classifying them: "Who are the zoot suiters? Frankly—we do not know."[30] But in their very elusiveness can be found one of the more expressive statements on the psychology of adolescence and the mentality of the home front.

Zoot-suiters were nonsensical because among other things they took pride in their ambiguity. The narcissistic self-absorption of the zoot-suiter in a world of illusory omnipotentiality was in opposition to the modesty of individual selflessness attributed to the defense worker and the soldier. Zoot-suiters transgressed the patriotic ideals of commitment, integrity, and loyalty with noncommitment, incoherence, and defiance. They seemed to be simply marking time while the rest of the country intensified the war effort. If there was a commitment, it was to nothing more enduring than sporting the zoot-suit way of life, with the emphasis on exhibiting themselves and indulging in their favorite forms of entertainment. As to past and future, they had few opinions. However irksome to adults, the zoot-suiters' flair for marking time—a characteristic richly conveyed through their animated contrariness—was a healthy and appropriate phase in the process of maturation.

Erik Erikson was the first to delineate the psychodynamics of the adolescent phase of marking time. In his concept of the moratorium is found the range of youthful activities that led to either a successful transition to adulthood or an interminable struggle against regressive impulses. Among Erikson's many eloquent passages is this one pertaining to young Martin Luther, but it is of value to understanding youth in general:

> Finally, the use of sharp repudiation, so eagerly indulged in by intolerant youth in an effort to bolster its collective identity with a harsh denunciation of some other

"kind," be it on a religious, racial, or social basis, is blunted in such a person. He alternates between extreme self-repudiation and a snobbish disdain for all groups—except perhaps, for memberships whose true roots and obligations are completely outside his reach. One thinks of the "classical" yearning of young Europeans or of the appeal which foreign totalitarian parties have for some young Americans, as do the lofty teachings of Eastern mystics. Here the need to search for total and final values can often be met only under the condition that these values be foreign to everything one has been taught.[31]

The moratorium is a period of experimentation, psychic restructuring, and a search for identity. A major phase of the moratorium is seen in the development of a negative identity: "We will call all self-images, even those of a highly idealistic nature, which are diametrically opposed to the dominant values of an individual's upbringing, parts of a negative identity—meaning an identity which he has been warned not to become."[32]

The explanatory value of the psychodynamics of adolescent moratoria and negative identity were not available to social commentators in the 1940s. For them, as indeed for the general public, the zoot-suiters' rejection of traditional values was insufferably irreverent and bordered on the profane. But the zoot-suiter image was somewhat traditional. The teens, twenties, and thirties of the twentieth century withstood the excesses of libertines and bohemians, just as the 1950s managed the intrusion of the beatnik and the 1960s that of the hippies, yippies, and a slew of minority dissidents that included Chicanos, blacks, and women. But no amount of tradition could convince the average American of the normality of zoot-suiters or pachucos.

The intolerance of adults could well be traced to a legacy of socio-economic oppression and political insensitivity to the realities of ethnic and working-class minorities. The difficulty with understanding the plight of the adolescent was unfortunately more complex than the conflictual struggles between classes and races. The one experience common to all classes and races is that of understanding their children. The majority of adult Anglos were no more tolerant of the pachuco than adult Anglos were of the zoot-suiters. Even those who by profession are presumed to be tolerant of youth are often as intolerant as the therapeutically mindless parent. An honest sample from nationally recognized Peter L. Giovacchini, a psychoanalyst, is illustrative: "Sometimes, the therapist views the patient's behavior as rebellious, and for some mysterious reason, adolescent rebellion is the worst kind. Passive rebellion, manifested by procrastination, is particularly irksome.''[33] Giovacchini's concept of adolescent procrastination is a variant of Erikson's moratorium.

The adolescent, even as a patient in a controlled therapeutic environment, is understandably overwhelmed by the avalanche of intellectual, emotional, and physical changes that prepare youth for the tasks of adulthood. In the midst of transacting these involuntary processes adolescents lack the coherence and experience to communicate much more than the obvious and painful realities of passing through adolescence.

Historians have sidestepped adolescent communications in much the same manner that mental health practitioners have opted for the more controllable and predictable treatment of childhood and adult neuroses. The language of adolescence in general, much less the language of youth groups, has eluded the classificatory traditions of scholars. The reasons are legion and point to issues of generational conflict, authoritarianism, envy, etc. The bedrock conflict may rest with adult expectations of adolescents. Adults readily assume that the physical maturation of adolescents confers equivalent emotional and intellectual abilities. But there is nothing spontaneous about the stormy passage from adolescence to adulthood.

In order to earn membership in the covenant of elders it is often necessary for adolescents to undergo rites of passage. A religiously sanctioned example is the bar or bas mitzvah, in which the thirteen-year-old is initiated into adulthood. University fraternities and sororities practice hazing rituals that have led to injuries and fatalities. Herbert A. Block and Arthur Niederhoffer noted in *The Gang* (1959) that "Pachuco boys are reputed to perform outstanding deeds in violation of the law in order to gain admission to the gang."[34] The connection between the adolescent moratorium, negative identity, and ritual ordeals is inseparable from the processes of adolescent maturation. Each of these phases is a dynamic formulation on the adolescents' road to achieving mastery of their minds, bodies, and environment. While to adults the zoot-suiters represented the epitome of childish irresponsibility and immaturity, for the zoot-suiters the bizarre clothing, music, dances, and inventive neologisms were all indicative of the adolescent struggle for identity. Although the zoot-suiters stimulated thoughts about nihilism, the fad itself allowed them to proudly designate their studied superiority over adults: They could dance longer and better than adults, they were decidedly more colorful and creative in their clothing, and through their privileged argot they countered the mysteries of adult conventions. The brash effrontery of the zoot-suiters was but a variant of the universally recognized adolescent illusion of omnipotentiality.

If adolescents appeared unpardonably childish to adults, it was not long before the infantilizing effects of wartime produced a rash of regressive symptoms in adults. The very indecisiveness of war encouraged adults to abandon peacetime norms of behavior. It allowed and often forced them to temporize, delay, and surrender their identities—like the adolescents did in a passing fad—to the whim of external forces. Americans were motivated to consider new forms of imagery and symbolizations. In the absence of an unseen enemy they were invited to indulge their fantasies with a host of surrogate experiences. Cartoonists, filmmakers, and radio personalities saturated the public with vivid portrayals of real and imagined enemies. For the American home front, more so than for any of the other nations at war, there was a pressing need for a vicarious sense of direct participation in the war. Aside from the exigencies of mobilizing and sustaining a mood of patriotism, there was the obvious need of entertaining the public. Were Americans ready for realism or escapism? Hollywood quickly established the overwhelming preference for the latter.[35] The needs of adults, whether civilian or military, were central to the conduct and success of the war. The problem was that these needs were often nonverbal and inaccessible to the assumptions of the nation's leadership.

If it is agreed that youths have to be initiated into the tasks of adulthood, then how were adults initiated into the tasks of wartime? Like adolescents, adults had to experiment and negotiate a series of unfamiliar and stressful ordeals. And like adolescents, adults exhibited an initial effrontery and exuberance that was largely impulsive and therefore of short duration. California in particular had a long history of vigilante behavior. During the war some civilians renewed the tradition with some modifications as they undertook the defense of their state by providing and complicating the duties of safeguarding the state against enemy submarines, airplanes, and saboteurs. Those not directly involved in defense-related jobs augmented their patriotism by participating in volunteer organizations, thereby further enhancing their sense of directly participating in the war. Given the nature of wartime, any sense of belonging was transitory and subject to the unexpected. But these activities granted the participant, if nothing else, a momentary sense of direction and perhaps a feeling of mastery. Adults, too, had to be initiated into the responsibilities of a new identity. Where the adolescents found structure in clothes, music, and dances, the adults (along with many youths) found a similar outlet in bond drives, patriotic rallies, volunteer organizations, etc.

Servicemen likewise faced a series of initiatory ordeals. Foremost among these were the rituals of being inducted into military service. There were oaths of loyalty and symbolic steps to be taken and a host of physical obstacles to be overcome, beginning with the stripping of their civilian clothes, hair, and identity. Recruits were then passed through another series of obstacle courses—physical and emotional—having to do with military drill, discipline, and plain harassment. Ironically, most servicemen never saw combat. Yet, as will become evident, it was crucial for the identity, well-being, and adaptation of Americans in general to entertain thoughts of having been exposed to the enemy.

There were several areas where the emotional experiences of servicemen, civilians, and zoot-suiters came together. Instead of representing disparate elements in the social history of Los Angeles, these three rather amorphous and at times mutually exchangeable groups represented different approaches to a similar if not identical set of circumstances.

First there was the initiatory process of becoming part of a distinct cohort—a distinct group tainted by a unique cluster of events. All three were confronted with certain rites of passage. For zoot-suiters it meant initiation into a formal gang or, at a less formal level, a voluntary initiation into an adolescent fad calling for the incorporation of specific mannerisms, linguistic protocols, and attire. For civilians it could mean a transfiguration into the novel status of "citizensoldier" on the home front, and its attendant duties and status. These could range from forsaking wage increases in deference to the impositions of wartime to experimenting with new forms of solidarity in the service of maintaining social order. Similar conditions and demands held for young men in basic training. It was here that all three groups often came together, unknowingly and inexorably. All recruits had been civilians, some were zoot-suiters, some were average adolescents, some were workers, and some were adults who were both workers and zoot-suiters. All three groups shared the anguish and euphoria of being caught in a transitional epoch.

The undifferentiated melding of anxieties, frustrations, and expectations suggests a point of psychosocial convergence that affected the unconscious and conscious processes of a people in the center of massive psychic and physical upheaval. Whatever the historical antecedents of zoot-suiters, workers, or youth in general, the uncompromising demands of a world war forced the great majority to move away from thinking of life in terms of moderation and to consider the extremes of immortality or oblivion. Thus zoot-suiters were thrusted into a political scene that was both alien and unprecedented. They succumbed to the psychological totalism of a time calling for the imperatives of either total patriotism or total disloyalty. But zoot-suiters could not be both good Americans and good pachucos. And neither, for that matter, could servicemen be good soldiers and theoretically have reservations about the course of the war. The same held for civilians whose presumed loyalty superceded all self-interests. The Zoot-Suit Riots signify one of the ways in which all of the taboos of homefront America could be contravened, and it is here, and not in the history of either Mexican-American youth, servicemen, or civilians, that the riots take on center stage in the social history of World War II America.

2. The Sleepy Lagoon Case

Early in the war, coastal cities like Los Angeles were often beset by mass fears of being attacked or infiltrated by the enemy. The resounding success of Nazi Fifth Columnists in Europe led many to envision similar catastrophes in the United States. In California the major concern was with Japanese and Japanese Americans. Unlike other parts of the country, Californians had a long history of directing legislation, vigilante activities, and general antipathy toward the Japanese. Although the Japanese identified with and had internalized the American dream through their hard work, success, and assimilation of American ways, they remained virtually unknown to Californians save through stereotypes.

The events of 7 December 1941 added new dimensions to the way Californians perceived the Japanese. Instead of the usual complaint that they threatened the economy because of their willingness to do more for less, they became a military threat. Reports of lurking submarines off the coast, of Fifth Column activities, and even of Japanese infantry units poised for attack within the state were common. In the publics mind Japanese and Japanese Americans were indistinguishable physically and ideologically. As the image of the Japanese came into military and civilian focus there were exaggerations that at times came close to delusional and hallucinatory behavior. One celebrated example occurred in Los Angeles on 26 February 1942.

Late in the evening of the twenty-sixth, the United States Army sounded an alert about unidentified approaching aircraft. The conclusion was that Los Angeles was under air attack and searchlights scanned the skies for two hours while antiaircraft batteries fired hundreds of rounds. The *Los Angeles Times* gave this report:

> Roaring out of a brilliant moonlit western sky, foreign aircraft flying both in large formation and singly flew over Southern California early today and drew heavy barrages of anti-aircraft fire—the first ever to sound over United States continental soil against an enemy invader.[1]

The public response to the raid was unique, for there was no stampede to man the beaches against the invader nor was there a move to flee the city from the danger of continued bombardment. Instead, there was an obvious and pervasive pride in the feeling of having been the first city and civilian population in the United States to be attacked by the enemy. The absence of material evidence that an attack had indeed taken place did not shake the convictions of a city elevated to prominence by the alleged raid. However, "exultation turned to outrage the next day when the secretary of the Navy said there had been no enemy planes at all."[2] The secretary's words, intended to clarify the events of 26 February and perhaps to soothe public fears of the risks they faced, were met with a chorus of disbelief. "The Army, being thus accused of shooting up an empty sky, was outraged. Los Angeles authorities were outraged, especially the sheriff, who had valiantly helped the FBI round up numerous Japanese nurserymen and gardeners who were supposedly caught in the act of signalling the enemy planes."[3] In his summation of "The Great Los Angeles Air Raid," *Los Angeles Times* columnist Jack Smith wrote that "there was no aircraft carrier. There were no Zeros. There were no bombs. There was no raid. But it was a glorious night, if only a dream."[4]

Smith's use of the word "dream" was not an effort to interpret the psychodynamics of the event. It has more in common with the dictionary sense of the word that denotes a series of images, perceptions, visions, or feelings of a transitory nature that take place while asleep or while awake in a daydream. The "dreamlike" quality of the air raid was that it was in fact unreal. There was no air raid. The temptation then is to discount the event as having any historical meaning. Yet the response of Los Angelenos to the alleged air raid was physically and psychologically real. There was an attraction to their collective experience that held special significance for the citizenry of Los Angeles, the state of California, and perhaps the nation.

The most fascinating aspect of the Los Angeles air raid myth was the pride people felt in the idea of having been attacked. The more predictable wartime experience was a reaction of panic, horror, and flight when the threat or experience of enemy bombardment materialized. Londoners and Berliners may have rallied to the defense of their cities from aerial bombing, but these attacks were initially met with deep foreboding. In Los Angeles the emotional intensity came not from the attack itself, but from the general reaction against the secretary of the navy, who publicly announced there had been no raid. Despite oft-repeated concerns with being attacked or infiltrated by the Japanese, the city's demeanor after the "raid" had more in common with a festive atmosphere than with the more commonly expected reactions of heightened anxiety seen in air raid survivors. Instead of inducing feelings of hysteria, the air raid seemed to integrate and focus the sentiments of Los Angelenos.

The illusion of having been attacked was a powerful rallying symbol. It conferred a special status on the city as the first to come under enemy attack. Besides the surface notoriety that it brought, it also bestowed the city with the knowledge of the insider—one who had experienced a privileged and special event and could now claim to have known the enemy in combat. The idea of directly experiencing contact with the enemy has multiple and long-standing significance. In Los Angeles this also manifested itself in the behavior of pachucos. During and after the Zoot-Suit Riots Mexican-American youth were known to have shaven their heads—a kind of scarification that indicated their victimization by servicemen. These youngsters sported their smooth pates as a badge, meaning they had survived contact with their enemy. An equivalent process operated in the tenacious belief by civilians and military personnel that the city had been attacked and that they had survived this initiatory trial into combat.

The trials of wartime for civilians and soldiers alike changed so rapidly that there was a lag between an event and the literary representation of the event. The brutal experience of a world war caught the public unprepared. The idiom of the "Great Air Raid" was insecure and a testimonial to a public in conflict between a heartfelt desire to abide by the restraining guidelines of government edicts on how to comport themselves during the war and an equally heartfelt desire to exert control over their own lives. However much the rituals, rites, and ceremonies of wartime America aimed at rallying the public to the crusade against the Axis, most Americans knew that there were many areas of endeavor from which they were of necessity excluded. Events like the air raid offered Americans of every class, race, and religious and political affiliation an opportunity to assume command of one segment of the war. The response to the air raid demonstrated the manner in which the home front could construct and define its response to combating an unseen enemy.

The spontaneous, noninstitutional, nonrational, and nonmediated emotional processes that accentuated the uniqueness of the participants and freed them from conforming to the roles designated by national, state, and local leaders go counter to the more traditional sources of evidence that stress planned, rational, institutional, and mediated behavior. The air raid belongs to a class of events that has often eluded the classificatory methods of social scientists. Rather than identifying a series of concrete hard facts, the air raid points to an area of experience where the predominant activities were transitory, emotional, and, at least on the surface, seemingly impulsive. It nevertheless gave coherence to a group of people who came together under their own aegis. Whether these events were real or not was secondary to the flowering of what Victor Turner describes as the process of "communitas."[5] Communitas identifies the group's release from the formal structures of society. It is antistructural for it lies outside the conventions of institutional and traditional norms of order. To an important extent the concept of communitas represents the externalized form of the internal experiences of a group. Communitas generates a plethora of images and symbols and lacks the cognitive qualities associated with structured relationships. In the case of the air raid there was an effusion of spontaneity that was rational in the minds of Los Angelenos. This collective reaction to the confusion caused by the war was a form of controlled social disorder and served to restore a sense of order that normally would have been the function of the instituted structure. Thus when the secretary of the navy as the spokesman for the established order refuted claims of an air raid, it merely served to heighten the level of confusion and encouraged an unofficial view that was more congruent with the mood of the citizenry. According to Turner, the ongoing dialectic between structure and antistructure is an essential feature of society: "Society (societas) seems to be a process rather than a thing—a dialectical process with successive phases of structure and communitas. There would seem to be—if one can use such a controversial term—a human 'need' to participate in both modalities."[6]

A norm in any society is therefore an ongoing tension between structure and communitas. Surely tensions would increase in time of war when normative structures are tested and strained by extraordinary pressures. The interpretation of the air raid as an example of homefront communitas suggests something more dynamic than an impulsive hysterical mob reaction to the sound of unidentified aircraft over Los Angeles and something less than an institutionally sanctioned form of behavior. It is within this "betwixt and between" (to borrow from Turner) transitional state that a series of events leading to the Zoot-Suit Riots occurs.

The response to this non-air raid by Los Angelenos imposed order and conferred a sense of mastery over the chaotic and fragmentary experience of war. Although it is often and correctly assumed that war mobilizes and coalesces the national will, it also induces deeply felt misgivings and anxieties. A great number of Americans underwent a variety of profound emotional trials. Among the more familiar was that of leaving home, entering basic training, becoming a soldier, going to a war zone, experiencing combat, being emotionally and physically wounded, and then returning home to a civilian status. With this matrix came other harsh realities. Middle-class white youth suddenly found themselves stripped of their socioeconomic status, shouldering arms with working-class folk, the scion of recent immigrants, perhaps of a different ethnic or racial background. White male workers had to accommodate the discomfort if not open rage of having to work with the thousands of blacks and women who had entered the work force, while working longer hours for less pay. There were countless variations on the theme of transition throughout the country. For civilians in Los Angeles during the night of the "Great Air Raid" the transition was the acutely condensed experience of going from civilian to combatant and back to civilian in one night. The spontaneity of this mass public outcry underscored a predisposition on the part of many Americans to externalize their anxieties by way of relatively controlled and largely symbolic displays of social disorder. At time these displays were so distorted that they resembled the established ways of maintaining order. One of the better examples can be found in the Sleepy Lagoon trial.

Carey McWilliams may have felt there was something contagious about Hollywood: "In Los Angeles, where fantasy is a way of life, it was a foregone conclusion that the Mexicans would be substituted as the major scapegoat group once the Japanese were removed."[7] As proof, he offered the newsmedia's sudden preoccupation with features on Mexican crime. The popular meaning of scapegoatism, and perhaps the definition McWilliams had in mind, is consonant with the psychoanalytic concept of displacement, in which aggression is transferred from one object to a more distant one. In the eyes of contemporaries, the hostility directed against the Mexican-American community was either indicative of the criminality, disloyalty, and unassimilability of Mexicans, or was another instance of racism, xenophobia, and mass displacement. These contrary sentiments became increasingly rigid during 1942 and 1943 as confrontations between Anglos and Mexicans were made public by the press. Although they were often characterized by violence and rage, these encounters demonstrated levels of symbolization inherent to communitas and liminality. At least one of the ordeals, the Sleepy Lagoon trial, exemplified the dynamics of communitas, but was carried out through the institution of a court of law.

The Sleepy Lagoon case and the air raid have many similarities of which the most outstanding is the fact that the central event did not occur. Neither the allegation that a murder was committed nor the attack on Los Angeles by the Japanese was ever proven. A major difference was that the Sleepy Lagoon case involved formal procedures. Yet these procedures themselves assumed the traits of antistructure and liminality as degradation ceremonies, ordeals of humiliation, and a variety of initiatory processes were introduced into the proceedings.

The ordeal began with what at another time may have been nothing more disruptive than one of the many manslaughter cases investigated and tried in Los Angeles. In August 1942 the body of José Díaz was found on a south-central city road. The proximity of the mortally wounded Díaz to a ranch where several Mexican-American adolescents had scuffled on the preceding night led to the mass arrest of suspected gang members. McWilliams claimed that up to 600 were rounded up and questioned on suspicion of having murdered Díaz. The alleged crime had occurred near a swimming hole dubbed Sleepy Lagoon by Mexican-American youngsters who were prevented from using the segregated public pools. "Sleepy Lagoon" was the name of a popular Henry James tune and also of a movie. Chicano historian Rodolfo Acuña concurred with McWilliams in citing scapegoating as the prime motive behind the exaggerated response to the case. Acuña adds that "the Sleepy Lagoon defendants became the prototype of the Mexican hoodlum as portrayed in the press."[8] Until the advent of the Sleepy Lagoon case Mexican-American youth had not been the focus of either widespread police or journalistic investigation.

The death of José Díaz occasioned a mass trial in which seventeen Mexican-American youth were convicted of and imprisoned for murder. The trial itself was a contravention of normal judicial procedures. McWilliams, although hardly impartial, gave an account that was in fact corroborated by the Second District Court of Appeals in 1944. According to McWilliams:

> It [the trial] took place before a biased and prejudiced judge (found to be such by an appellate court); it was conducted by a prosecutor who pointed to the clothes and the style of haircut of the defendants as evidence of guilt; and was staged in an atmosphere of intense community-wide prejudice which had been whipped up and artfully sustained by the entire press of Los Angeles.
>
> From the beginning the proceedings savored more a ceremonial lynching than a trial in a court of justice. The defendants were not allowed to sit with their counsel—there were seven defense attorneys—and were only permitted to communicate with them during recesses and after adjournment. For the first weeks of the trial, the defendants were not permitted to get haircuts and packages of clean clothes were intercepted by the jailer on orders of the prosecutor. As a consequence of this prejudicial order, the defendants came trouping into the courtroom every day looking like so many unkempt vagabonds.[9]

The prosecution had clearly accentuated the criminality and marginality of Mexican youth.

The case centered on the accusation of a conspiracy to commit murder. Díaz had allegedly died as a result of injuries sustained after a group of party crashers fought at the Williams ranch near the Sleepy Lagoon. George Shibley, chief counsel for eight of the defendants, recalled the charge:

> The conspiracy was a conspiracy or an agreement to commit a trespass. In other words, when these twenty-two or forty-two young men and women said, "let's go crash the party," or "let's go to the Williams ranch," whether they said it in words or by assent in just joining the group, they were agreeing or conspiring to commit a misdemeanor.[10]

Since an alleged felony had been committed during the "conspiracy," all of the young men were charged with murder in the first degree. According to Shibley, the case for a conspiracy was applicable only if a court of law accepted the concept of a "conspiracy to crash a party" as proof of felonious intent. A court of law did, and on 12 January 1943 convictions of second-degree murder were handed down on nine of the defendants, first-degree murder on three, with five being convicted on lesser charges.

The Sleepy Lagoon case gained fame for the extraordinary judicial procedures used and the bizarre nature of the evidence brought before the court. One of the stronger efforts to discredit Mexicans came from Lieutenant Edward Duran Ayres of the sheriff's department in testimony before the grand jury. Ayres presented a discourse on genetics in making a case for the racial determinants responsible for Mexican juvenile delinquency and violence. He directed the grand jury's attention to the oriental background of Mexico's pre-Columbian ancestors, underscoring their mutual disregard for human life: ". . . the Indian, from Alaska to Patagonia, is evidently Oriental in background—at least he shows many of the oriental characteristics, especially so in his utter disregard for the value of life."[11] Referring to Aztec human sacrifice, Ayres added: "This total disregard for human life has always been universal throughout the Americas among the Indian population, which of course is well known to everyone."[12] Ayres completed the syllogism connecting Oriental atavism with Mexican violence in the United States with the following:

> They [Mexican authorities] have stated that which we are now learning the hard way. The Mexican Indian is mostly Indian—and that is the element which migrated to the United States in such large numbers and looks upon leniency by authorities as an evidence of weakness or fear, or else he considers that he was able to outsmart the authorities.[13]

Ayres displayed his own antistructural and anti-institutional leanings by recommending dispensing with due process. "It is just as essential to incarcerate every member of a particular gang, whether there be ten or fifty, as it is to incarcerate one or two of the ringleaders."[14] His most ambitious proposal was to advise in favor of retroactive punishment. "The time to rehabilitate them is both before and after the crime has been committed . . ."[15] Mexican youth were to be kept in a state of perpetual liminality—always marginal and bereft of social status. This eternal infantilization applied, by implication, to all Mexicans of all ages. Ayres drew on metaphor to illustrate his point:

> Although a wild cat and domestic cat are of the same family, they have certain biological characteristics so different that while one may be domesticated, the other would have to be caged to be kept in captivity, and there is practically as much difference between the races of man . . .[16]

Another example of Ayres's partiality for feline allegories: "In fact, as mentioned above, economics as well as some of the other features are contributing factors [to Mexican delinquency], but basically it is biological—one cannot change the spots of a leopard."[17]

The Ayres report portrayed Mexican Americans and Mexicans as a tainted people condemned to racial inferiority and social and economic marginality. This argument was familiar to Nazis who perceived Americans as a mongrelized race. Jews, blacks, Asians, Indians, Europeans, and Hispanics were part of the "melting pot." The biological determinism presented by Ayres aligned him with the core of Nazi racial theories. Unlike a 1942 Gallup poll that found Mexicans slightly more acceptable to Americans than Japanese, Ayers contrasted the law-abiding Chinese and Japanese with the violence-prone Mexicans—momentarily severing the tie between violence and Orientals. Ayres crossed the line from communitas to structure by proposing that certain measures be institutionalized into the procedures for dealing with Mexican-American youth. He suggested that gangs be taken out of "circulation" and that "all those under eighteen who will not attend school should work, and even if they do work, if they resort to such criminal acts as evidenced lately by these gangs, then they should be incarcerated where they must work under supervision and discipline."[18] An even worse fate awaited the eighteen-year-old: "All those eighteen years of age and over should be found a place in the armed forces of our country at this time."[19] In peacetime it was common to use military service as a rehabilitation alternative for wayward but not incorrigible youth. But in wartime military service is imbued with the ritual and emotional significance reserved for a class of youth entrusted by virtue of their innocence and purity with the task of defending the nation. Obviously this was an illusion, but Ayres's recommendations went against the dominant view of the recruit as a clean-cut all-American athlete from the countryside. It also portrayed the armed forces as a reprieve for the unwanted.

The subtle degradation of military service by Ayres was symptomatic of a pervasive ambivalence toward groups and institutions that had gained visibility and ascendancy during the war. Ayres's association about juvenile delinquency led him to think about the military. His discomfort with the difficulties of dealing with adolescents epitomized part of a generalized frustration with individuals, groups, and events that did not conform to expectation. Youth were unpredictable as indeed were the realities of home front and battlefront America. Ayres's dissatisfaction, together with that of the prosecution, public opinion, and Judge Fricke, led to one of the more enduring coalitions between Mexicans, Jews, blacks, and Anglos in American history.

The conviction of the Sleepy Lagoon defendants brought about the formation of the Sleepy Lagoon Defense Committee. The committee was an outgrowth of the Citizen's Committee for the Defense of Mexican-American Youth. The latter in turn had been organized to prepare an appeal on the convictions tendered by the grand jury against the Sleepy Lagoon defendants. With the formation of the Sleepy Lagoon Defense Committee came the support of a national cross-section of American interest groups and organizations. Among the sponsors were representatives from the International Workers Order, International Longshoremen's and Warehousemen's Union, Council for Pan American Democracy, the Screen Office Employees Guild, American Newspaper Guild, Screen Artist's Guild, Lawyer's Guild, Congress of Industrial Workers, Amalgamated Clothing Workers Union of America, and National Maritime Union of America. Carey McWilliams chaired the Sleepy Lagoon Defense Committee with the support of LaRue McCormick, Alice Greenfield, Josefina Fierro de Bright, Orson Welles, Anthony Quinn, Rita Hayworth, Bert Corona, and Mrs. Will Rogers, Jr.

Through the committee a powerful and coordinated response to the conviction of the Sleepy Lagoon defendants was launched that resulted in the dismissal of the charges and the release of the defendants in October 1944. The committee took the offensive by charging that it was the grand jury, Judge Charles W. Fricke, and particularly the testimony presented by Lieutenant Ayres that represented a threat from within to the nation's survival. Where nativism before had been defined as the un-American activities of a foreign element (usually Catholics, Jews, and Communists) operating within the United States, the committee redefined nativism as the alleged activities of pro-American groups as seen in the work of the Hearst press and the Los Angeles Grand Jury that convicted the Sleepy Lagoon defendants. According to the committee, the exaggerated Americanism of the Hearst press et al., was a ruse orchestrated by the Axis. Guy Endore's *The Sleepy Lagoon Mystery* (1944) proposed a conspiratorial theory in which the Hearst press emerged as the principal saboteur of American war aims. Without identifying his sources, Endore offered "evidence" indicating that the harassment and persecution of Mexicans was part of a Nazi design to topple American war morale and eventually to create internal discord. The machinations of the Hearst press encouraged the police, the public, and the Los Angeles Grand Jury to consider the fringes of Nazi ideology: "For with the best intentions in the world, the Grand Jury only succeeded in becoming the nucleus from which spread out the horrific tales of race degeneracy, racial criminality, and other Hitleristic concepts."[20] As further proof, Endore quoted Hitler: " 'It will be a simple matter for me,' Hitler told [Hermann] Rauschning, 'to produce unrest and revolt in the United States, so that these gentry will have their hands full with their own troubles.' "[21] The allegations of collaboration between the Third Reich and the Hearst press accentuated the argument that the accused Mexican youth were innocent Americans deprived of their constitutional rights. Later the Sleepy Lagoon case and the Zoot-Suit Riots were seen by well-intentioned Chicanos as symbolic of the beginning of the Chicano movement, thereby ironically siding with the prosecution's charge that the Sleepy Lagoon defendants were separatists and a threat to American security. The Sleepy Lagoon Defense Committee had assiduously argued against the implication of any separatist or un-American activities on behalf of either Mexicans or Mexican Americans.

In *The Sleepy Lagoon Case* (1944), a collectively written committee pamphlet with a foreword by Orson Welles, the immediate basis for American-Mexican cooperation was made clear:

> . . . above all we need Mexicans, all the Mexicans in the United States. Some of them came here long ago, to build our railroads and cultivate our fields. Some came in 1917, to help us win another war. And now [1944] thousands more are coming in answer to our call for help. We need them now to take the place of our boys gone to the fighting fronts. But we need them also to take up with us the challenge thrown by Ed. Duran Ayres. We need all they bring us from their ancient culture, their long, proud, rich history.[22]

These sentiments were congruent with the needs of American propaganda: They served to dissolve class and race distinctions, appealed to the ideals of fraternity and equality, and took note of the contributions made by generations of Mexicans in the United States. One of the recurrent arguments of the committee was that the war was a unified effort by men of different races to once and for all dispel the myth of racial superiority: "Our coming victory on the continent of Europe will be won by 'men of the same stamp' though different races, and it will be the victory of all—Indians, Malays, Chinese, Negroes, Russians, Slavs, French, English, Americans, yes, and of Germans, Italians and Japanese."[23] Much of the egalitarian rhetoric of the committee reflected a benign acknowledgment of Communist party support: "And because this global war is everywhere a peoples' war, all of us are in it together, all of us together take up the challenge of Sleepy Lagoon."[24] Besides taking the offensive against the Axis, the committee pledged itself to fight "against the Sinarchists and the Falangists, and against every organized group, Mexican or American, that tries to disrupt our unity."[25] There was a melting pot tangent to the committee's political sentiments. Indeed, in some of their pronouncements they practically wedded Mexicans and Anglo Americans:

> "Hidalgo and Juárez were men of the same stamp as Washington and Jefferson," President Roosevelt said. "It was therefore inevitable that our two countries should find themselves aligned together in the great struggle which is being fought today to determine whether this shall be a free world or a slave world." So, too, it is inevitable that all of us should fight together in the case of Sleepy Lagoon.[26]

The sympathies of the committee were bona fide expressions of communal solidarity. However effective the support of the committee and its Anglo and Mexican sponsors, racism increased in the years that followed and undid some of the work of these individuals and organizations. Although the integrity of the judicial system was restored with the reversal of the Sleepy Lagoon convictions in the fall of 1944, the allegations about Mexican-American delinquency became more widespread.

One of the foremost impressions generated by the trial was for the need to defend the United States from foreign and internal enemies. There was little physical evidence to support the charge of either Japanese or Nazi infiltration of the west coast in late 1942 (although rumors of lurking Japanese submarines continued until after the war). The Sleepy Lagoon trial provided a substitute hate object for a home front where the real enemy was too distant and beginning to retreat. The civilian surrogate war effort was a type of psychological luxury at a time when a real enemy was confronting the Allies. While the war evoked feelings of solidarity and communalism in one segment of the population, it likewise evoked the opposite sentiments of disintegration, catastrophe, and imminent annihilation in another segment. Richard Hofstadter made some observations about the mobilization of paranoia and the life of the authentic paranoid:

> . . . although they both tend to be overheated, oversuspicious, overaggressive, grandiose and apocalyptic in expression, the clinical paranoid sees the hostile and conspiratorial world in which he feels himself to be living as directed specifically *against him*; whereas the spokesman of the paranoid style finds it directed against a nation, culture, a way of life whose fate affects not himself alone but millions of others.[27]

Hofstader's distinctions between the private and public paranoid were an understandable misinterpretation of the psychodynamics of paranoia. Freud's classic analysis of the Schreber case demonstrated the connection between persecutory feelings in the individual and the delusional idea of saving the world.[28] But Hofstadter did recognize that the delusional behavior of the political paranoids could incite an equally delusional patriotism: "His sense that his political passions are unselfish and patriotic, in fact, goes far to intensify his feeling of righteousness and his moral indignation."[29] But no amount of moral indignation could rectify a distorted judgment: "A distorted style is, then, a possible signal that may alert us to a distorted judgment, just as in art an ugly style is a cue to fundamental defects in taste. What interests me here is the possibility of using political rhetoric to get at political pathology."[30] Significantly, the rhetoric of the Communist party often paralleled that of the Sleepy Lagoon's prosecution and of the Tenny Committee on Un-American Activities.

The political mission for the Communist party was to save Mexicans from a Fascist Sinarquista conspiracy—a goal similar to that of anti-Communists. LaRue McCormick, at whose suggestion the Citizens' Committee for the Defense of Mexican-American Youth had been formed, was unsparing in her contention that Mexican Sinarquista Fifth Columnists were responsible for the rise in juvenile delinquency. The tactic favored by Guy Endore was a mainstay of the Communist party and many of the supporters of the Sleepy Lagoon case. The logic was not to attack American institutions, but to attack foreign elements that threatened those institutions. By charging that the opponents of the Sleepy Lagoon defendants were inspired by Fascist propaganda and sentiments, Endore, McCormick, and McWilliams invoked the argument of nativism: the voluntary and planned organization of foreign elements within the United States for the purpose of overthrowing the government. And there was another implication. Unlike Lieutenant Ayres's candid conclusions about the atavism of Mexican delinquents, the Left and Right in California were incapable of acknowledging the existence of Mexican crime without linking it to an external guiding intelligence.

The mobilization by the Mexican-American community is generally lost in the broadsides between the Tenny Committee investigations of 1943 and those of the Communist party. The efforts of organizations like Cultura Pan Americana, the Coordinating Council for Latin American Youth, the Mexican Welfare Committee, the American-Mexican Victory Youth Club, and the Cleland House Athletic Club went largely unnoticed.

The impulsive and impressionistic publicity directed at the zoot-suiters set the stage for the making of an unambiguous Mexican. Whether spurred by primitive Aztec rituals, Communists, Sinarquistas, or Anglos, the zoot-suiters were anathema. In late 1942, the zoot-suiters became the backdrop against which a changing array of actors were contrasted and brought into brief public prominence.

The Sleepy Lagoon trial demonstrated reactions beyond those usually associated with racism. A pattern conditioned by the emotional push and pull of wartime upheaval was borne out by the trial. The practice of keeping the young defendants unkempt, dirty, and in their original clothes for days accentuated the foreignness of the defendants and made them appear extraordinarily bizarre and marginal. Many of the procedures initiated by the prosecution were stripping ceremonies in which the young pachucos were deprived of their identity, prestige, and self-reliance. The very status conferred by the zoot suit was transformed into a liability. The prosecution was uncompromising in its effort to heighten the primitive, archaic, and alien characteristics evoked by the defendants. The tactic of exhibiting them was not far removed from carnival freak shows and the display of deformities, aberrations, and the paraphernalia of criminals. These devices would have fizzled had there not been a public predisposed to suggestions about strange people and strange situations. The war was uncanny and it confronted the average American with thoughts about death, annihilation, and the unpredictable. Imminently related to these thoughts was a series of derivatives having to do with rebellion, murderous fantasies, feelings of persecution, and forbidden sexual desires. It is not surprising that the focus throughout the years of the zoot-suit mania was on allegations about endemic murdering, profligacy, and disloyalty.

The boundaries between the real enemy and imaginary enemies were fluid. Besides representing a fragmented and distorted version of the external enemy, the pachuco zoot-suiter also represented youth. War called for the sacrifice of youth in defense of the nation. In his monumental work *Suicides* (1979), Jean Baechler describes the specifics of institutionalized oblative suicide—suicide in defense of one's country—as an enduring characteristic of wartime. Indeed, many of the early war films such as *Guadalcanal, Bataan*, and *Back to Bataan* implicitly and explicitly addressed the question of self-sacrifice. There were no survivors in *Guadalcanal* or *Bataan*, and in *Back to Bataan* the central theme is atonement for the sacrifices of dead compatriots. One of the latent meanings of the Sleepy Lagoon trial may have been to offer a sacrifice in atonement for other youth lost in the war. This sentiment was made explicit in the recommendation that zoot-suiters be drafted and presumably sent to the war front. There was also an element of sacrifice from the point of view of the defendants themselves who colluded—probably unconsciously—with the demands of their prosecutors. By declining to testify against other members of their group, by refusing the offices of defense attorneys, and by forfeiting some of the rights of self-defense, they symbolically and physically sacrificed themselves.

The most immediate impact of the case was that it introduced a new way of thinking about zoot-suiters. They were bizarre creatures, somewhat fantastic, subterranean, clearly identifiable by their garb and argot, yet elusive and of uncertain origins. They represented a social anomaly; still they provoked anomalous behavior from the law-abiding citizen. They were vulnerable to the reproach of society, but at the same time zealously defended by righteous individuals and groups. Their detractors saw them as a sinister group capable of inflicting great moral and physical harm on society. Their defenders saw them as victims of a callously racist social structure. Clearly the strengths and weaknesses of the zoot-suiters were inventions that fed the sensibilities of their supporters as well as their detractors. But whether as social pariahs or innocent victims, the Sleepy Lagoon trial rendered the zoot-suiters nationally visible and provided a forum for the exchange of accusations, exhortations, and exonerations for individuals and special interest groups. As an object of scorn and idealization, the zoot-suiters defined an emotional and physical arena where polarized citizens converged in the spirit of communitas. The liminality of the pachuco zoot-suiter was preserved, but not in the historic sense of individuals with a linguistic and archetypal ancestry. Instead, the 1942 zoot-suiters were fashioned in accordance with the imagery and symbolization of the American home front. In the fantasies about zoot-suiters could be found an alternatively sublime warrior and a demented collaborator of the Axis. Thus zoot-suiters, previously insignificant or merely quixotic for the general public, were awarded a conditional status that was subject to the whim and convictions of their detractors and defenders.

It was very much like the theater of the absurd where everything is possible. It was also very much like the characteristics of unconscious behavior where everything too is possible. The dream of the "Great Air Raid" was dramatic proof of the mass illusory potential of a people undergoing the stress of wartime. The Sleepy Lagoon trial, with its suspension of judicial procedure, had demonstrated another dimension of this group process. In the months to come the zoot-suit image underwent further elaborations and reached a phantasmagoric zenith at the hands of Al Capp and his "Zoot-Suit Yokum" cartoon.

3. The "Zoot-Suit Yokum" Conspiracy

A behavioral characteristic of wartime is the ubiquity of conspiratorial thinking. Allied and Axis propagandists were quick to exploit the potential threat of enemy saboteurs, spies, Fifth Columnists, and sympathizers to the safety of their respective countries. Although most foreign agents were too professional to be uncovered by the untrained layman, the act of enlisting mass support in defense of the home front was a splendid means of arousing patriotism. The electrifying swoon of direct involvement in the war was contagious and could make the peacetime recluse bristle with martial fantasies of conquest.

In the United States the measure for identifying enemy sympathizers or agents was the telltale sign of un-American behavior. For example, during the Ardennes offensive of 1944 Nazi soldiers infiltrated the American lines dressed in GI uniforms and speaking flawless English, but they were detected when they failed to know a piece of Americana relating to sports. At the start of the war, race and to a lesser extent nationality were tests of un-Americanism. Thus Japanese Americans were quickly interned and removed from sight, although German Americans—physically indistinguishable from the general population despite Nazi claims to the contrary—were left relatively untouched. Another measure was simply to contrast "what America stood for" against select opponents. It therefore had been natural for both the supporters and detractors in the Sleepy Lagoon struggle to cast each other in the most pernicious roles, while upholding for themselves the loftier ideals of American liberty, freedom, and law.

Yet un-American behavior as typified by complex conspiracies seldom attracted sustained public interest. Imminently more volatile were the evocative symbols associated with long-standing bias. Antilabor and antiunion sentiments could readily be marshalled. Grieving workers risked accusations of seditious intent if levels of productivity and absenteeism went counter to government and public expectations. The movement of southern blacks into predominantly segregated industries in the North kindled fears of job displacement by whites whose lament rhymed with patriotism.   The re-emergent nativism of the war years was a continuation of prewar hysteria. Many brands of prejudice flourished concurrently with the effort against Nazi genetic determinism. But the United States was clearly neither the Third Reich nor given to the extreme propaganda needs of countries ravished by combat on native soil. The enemy, except for the days following the attack on Pearl Harbor and occasional rumors of lurking U-boats, was a remote entity for most homefront Americans. Propagandists enjoyed the luxury of symbolic license in stereotyping the "enemy." The somewhat relaxed needs of American propaganda allowed self-appointed patriots to render their unique versions of the evils confronting the nation. This was vividly seen in the creative arts where writers, artists, and actors rallied around the flag and functioned as official and unofficial envoys of government policy. One of the engrossing preoccupations of wartime popular culture was with the comic books and comic strips.

Comic books were a war novelty that reached a billion-dollar market in 1944.[1] Two distinct consumer groups grew during the war—"one for children, one for servicemen."[2] Together with newspaper comic strips, comic books absorbed much of the reading of Americans. Comics were a powerful psychological force in redirecting the anxieties, anger, horror, and frustration of wartime uncertainty. They simplified, titillated, and satirized where other mediums were checked by convention. They also provided the kind of aesthetic deception that was pleasing to the national ego. "In most comic strips, Americans won their battles alone, allies were nonexistent or subordinate, the enemy was a pushover."[3] Psychologists working for the Office of War Information lamented the fact that comic strip heroes, while acting with epic invincibility from the enemy assaults, were frightfully insensitive to the realities of a world at war.[4] Race prejudice, American chauvinism, and phobic statements about the Allies were common comic book fare. And for millions of Americans the comics were the major source of information—especially for those who read nothing else.[5] So effective were comic books as a propaganda medium that even the U.S. Office of War Information printed its own version—a memorable one being in the form of an attempted biography of Franklin Delano Roosevelt.[6] Comic books had a direct psychological and political impact on their audience. They reinforced stereotypical individuals, groups, and situations and tapped the basest emotions. Clearly, the comic book provided the reader with a kind of emotional gratification that was unavailable in the daily experience of home-front America. Through the comic book the reader could vicariously participate in the front lines in the Pacific and European theaters of war. The daily comic strips offered an intimate perusal of an event, a project, or a group with which readers became emotionally immersed and that assumed residence in their fantasy and conscious lives. Comic book heroes were frequently treated by their admirers, young and old, as real people. To kill off a popular hero was to court venomous replies from daily patrons.[7] Besides the humor, aesthetic pleasure, or emotional release derived from comic books, they also served as substitutes for having contact with highly idealized or despised people.

One of the first to perceive the interchangeability between fantasy and reality in the existence of the zoot-suiters was the famed and controversial cartoonist Al Capp. It may not be a breach of historical reality to suggest that more than any other individual or institution Capp was responsible for introducing the American public to the perils of zoot-suiterism. We get a notion of the widespread appeal of Li'l Abner, Capp's mainstay character, from the following assessment by David Manning White:

> In research which I conducted recently at the Communication Research Center of Boston University, we ascertained that the most popular comic strips, such as *Li'l Abner,* reach an audience of 50 million readers or more practically every day of the year.[8]

One conservative estimate noted that there were one billion readers of the daily and Sunday strips of *Li'l Abner.*[9]

Between 11 April 1943 and 23 May 1943, in most Sunday installments of this country's newspapers, Capp used Li'l Abner to portray a chapter in the brief life of "Zoot-Suit Yokum." According to one of Capp's biographers, the purpose of this chapter was to show that human beings are "hero-imitating animal[s]."[10] Capp's purpose in creating Li'l Abner's personality centered on his preoccupation with death:

> I think that man is interested in two or three things. He is interested in death; he is exhilarated by the thought of death. That's the basis of all the adventure of Li'l Abner. It is always a flirtation with death; it is always a triumph over something that we all know will eventually triumph over us. So that I think we get some escape in Li'l Abner from the final certainty.[11]

The mingling of "flirtation" with death brings out elements of the hysteria present in the Capp comic formulation. The teasing, provocative, disingenuous illusion of triumph over death and the constant repetition of these themes made the *Li'l Abner* series the third most popular comic strip during the war.[12] Another element not mentioned by Capp was his intense fascination with conspiratorial machinations. Bizarre plots would be hatched by rather nebulous characters that threatened the total annihilation of either the United States or the world. These portrayals again merged tightly with the preoccupations of a citizenry beset by the uncertainties and pressures of war.

Capp represented many of the persecutory defenses of American reactionary politics in his anti-intellectualism and insatiable need for a scapegoat.

> For thousands of years we've been trying to remove the inhumanity from humans. Well, it can't be removed and it is nonsense trying to. The trick is to give man someone to be inhuman to who enjoys it. The trouble is that when psychiatry discovers those rare and useful people who love being treated cruelly, we try to cure them instead of breeding more of them. What this country needs is a good five cent masochist.[13]

This parable, partly in jest no doubt, is applicable to Capp's creation of "Zoot-Suit Yokum"—a five-cent masochist through which Capp introduced the zoot-suit craze to the American public.

The "Zoot-Suit Yokum" chapter presents aficionados with a conspiracy—the conspiracy of the zoot-suit clothing manufacturers to take over the country politically and economically. The vehicle for this take-over: "Create a great national hero who performs incredible deeds of valor—always dressed in a Zoot-Suit."[14] Realizing that this was a dangerous assignment the protagonists embarked on a search for the "man with the lowest I.Q. in America."[15] After months of searching, the man was found dangling from a tree in Yellowstone National Park . . ."[16] In the subsequent interview Capp brings up the possibility of death: "My man—er—you *are* a man, aren't you?— You certainly aren't *imbecile* enough to accept a job that means risking death, everyday?"[17] Capp's anti-intellectualism surfaces in an assault on higher education. Clearly visible in the center of the "imbecile's" sweater is an emblazoned "H"—signifying Harvard. Even then the Harvard man is not the one with the "lowest I.Q. in the nation." That honor goes to the redoubtable Li'l Abner, who is promised fame and fortune at eight dollars a week. With this impish, self-effacing entrance, Li'l Abner becomes the focus of the story and adopts the "Zoot-Suit Yokum" identity, which "will make millions" for the zoot-suit clothing manufacturer.

Arthur Asa Berger, author of the first major study of Capp and *Li'l Abner,* noted the changing roles assigned to Abner:

> We can distinguish three different aspects of Abner's role: first, his role is that of fool, generally (or often) an artificial fool, in the employ of the rich and powerful; second, he functions, for the reader, as a victim who diverts the wrath of the gods (and, who makes the reader feel better by being so obviously stupid and inferior [*sic*] person); third, he is a tool who allows Capp to judge society.[18]

As a result of Zoot-Suit Yokum's valor while "nattily dressed in one of our latest zoot-suits—with a drape shape, reet pleat and stuff cuff," the country is swiftly becoming "zoot-suiter conscious."[19] In the first frame to the 19 May installment, Capp begins with this description:

> From Maine to California a fanatical type of hero worship has engulfed this once conservative nation. The object of all this adulation is "Zoot-Suit Yokum" who has upon innumerable occasions rushed to scenes of disaster all over the country—and with incredible, foolhardy courage, performed amazing feats of strength and heroism. Naturally "Zoot-Suit Yokum" had become the idol of all red blooded young Americans—and this idol-worship has led millions of men to imitate his peculiar costume, known as the "Zoot-Suit." Clothing stores report that there has been a mad rush to buy "Zoot-Suits"—while the regular men's clothing market has hit its worst slump in one hundred years.[20]

It would not be long before reality imitated the fantasy world of Al Capp. On 13 June 1943, the *Los Angeles Times* ran this feature: ". . . the federal government stepped into the local zoot-suit picture by obtaining an injunction against a downtown store restraining the sale of zooters' 'uniform'. . . "[21] On the same 19 May installment of *Li'l Abner,* Capp ran this headline in the third frame: "Governor Issues Order Banning Zoot Suit Wearers!!"[22] On 10 June the *Los Angeles Times* printed the response of the city council to the zoot-suit menace: "Ban on Freak Suits Studied by Councilmen."[23]

Although Capp was attempting to satirize reality, it was reality that followed his cues. The imagery introduced by Capp into the *Li'l Abner* comic strip banked on inciting pleasure in reading sadistic reports of murder and mutilation. We see this headline—"Wife Kills Husband!!" —followed by a brief but ghoulish dispatch: " 'He refused to wear a zoot suit'—she says!! 'I'm glad I shot him through the head six times.' "[24] Capp's fantasies on the "Zoot-Suit Mania," to use his phrase, antedate the Zoot-Suit Riots. The source of inspiration for Capp's creativity came from within the inner recesses of his psyche and not, as alluded by Berger, from his desire to give expression to the turmoil of the external world.

A significant appeal in the "Zoot-Suit Yokum" chapter may have been the conspiratorial angle given to the plot. Capp encouraged the illusion of an imminent Zoot-Suiter take-over of the country. The reader was thus invited to participate in the twin fantasies of being the persecuted and, in time, the persecutor. Capp could indulge the reader in identifying with feelings of impotence, paranoia, worthlessness, and inferiority and, conversely, in projecting feelings of omnipotence, aggression, narcissism, and superiority onto weak objects.

The tempo in any Capp series could change rapidly. By arranging a case of mistaken identity, the "conservative clothing manufacturers" had prevailed upon Gat Garson, a convicted look-alike "dead ringer" for Zoot-Suit Yokum, to commit a dastardly deed while masquerading as the real heroic Yokum. In a remarkable change of pace, Gat Garson manages to falsify the popularity of Zoot-Suit Yokum by redirecting the public's indignation against anyone and everything associated with a zoot-suit. In the final frame of the chapter, Capp orchestrates what may well have been one of the greatest preconscious stimulants to the riots. The following headlines are contrasted against a solid black background: "Last Zoot-Suit Factory Goes Bankrupt!" "Zoot-Suit Hating Mobs Continue to Smash up Zoot Suit Store!!" and finally, "Last Zoot-Suit Preserved by Smithsonian Institution To Go on Exhibit in 'Chamber of Horrors' Section!!"[25] The "Last Zoot-Suit" represented the complete annihilation of the zoot-suiters.

Capp offered his readers the cathartic pleasure of momentarily identifying with the inequities of his protagonists as they shuffled through daily narcissistic injuries and survived demonic conspiracies. He offered them a simple world of extremes populated by the bizarre:

> The characters in this story . . . are all grotesques and eccentrics of one sort or another. The zoot-suiters wear fantastic clothing; McGenius charges ten thousand dollars for every word of advice; the Harvard man is an ape; Abner is the stupidest person in the world; the leader of the conservative clothing manufacturers is bald, has a great big nose, and is a freak; and all the minor characters are grotesques.[26]

Capp's penchant for representational extremes is pervasive. "There is hardly any middle-range here; everyone is either rich or poor, zoot-suiter or conservative, genius or moron."[27] The qualities of misidentification, diffusion, and symbolic condensation are present in primitive art and the art of schizophrenics and young children. "The

The following Al Capp cartoons are reprinted from *Li'l Abner: A Study in American Satire* by Arthur Asa Berger, (Boston: Twayne Publishers, Inc., 1970).

"ZOOT SUIT" YOKUM

L-LOOK — **ANOTHER ONE.!!** —AND **ANOTHER ONE.!!**

THAT'S **SIX** WE'VE SEEN ON THIS BLOCK, ALONE.!!—IT'S A HORRIFYING THOUGHT—BUT, THERE ARE PROBABLY **MILLIONS** OF 'EM IN THE WORLD.!!

YES (SIGH.!)—WE MUST FACE IT.!! THERE MUST BE **MILLIONS** OF MEN IN THIS COUNTRY WHO **DON'T** WEAR **ZOOT SUITS.!!**

WE MUST IMPROVE THAT SHOCKING SITUATION! OUR GOAL MUST BE—**A ZOOT SUIT ON EVERY MAN OR BUST.!!**

WE **MUST** MAKE THIS NATION ZOOT SUIT CONSCIOUS.!! WE MUST MAKE IT SEEM A SOCIAL CRIME **NOT** TO WEAR ONE.—BUT, **HOW?**

WE'LL HIRE J. COLOSSAL McGENIUS, THE GREAT **"IDEA MAN"** TO FIGURE OUT A WAY.!! HIS ADVICE COSTS **TEN THOUSAND DOLLARS A WORD** —BUT IT'S WORTH IT.!!—

ENTIRE NATION GRIPPED BY ZOOT-SUIT MANIA!!

ZOOT-SUIT YOKUM

FROM MAINE TO CALIFORNIA A FANATICAL TYPE OF HERO WORSHIP HAS ENGULFED THIS ONCE CONSERVATIVE NATION. THE OBJECT OF ALL THIS ADULATION IS "ZOOT-SUIT YOKUM" WHO HAS, UPON INNU-MERABLE OCCASIONS, RUSHED TO SCENES OF DISASTER ALL OVER THE COUNTRY – AND, WITH INCREDIBLE, FOOLHARDY COURAGE, PERFORMED AMAZING FEATS OF STRENGTH AND HEROISM. NATURALLY, "ZOOT-SUIT YOKUM" HAS BECOME THE IDOL OF ALL RED-BLOODED YOUNG AMERICANS – AND THIS IDOL-WORSHIP HAS LED MILLIONS OF MEN TO IMITATE. HIS PECULIAR COSTUME, KNOWN AS THE "ZOOT SUIT." CLOTHING STORES REPORT THAT THERE HAS BEEN A MAD RUSH TO BUY "ZOOT SUITS" – WHILE THE REGULAR MEN'S CLOTHING MARKET HAS HIT ITS WORST SLUMP IN ONE HUNDRED YEARS.

NON-ZOOT-SUIT WEARER RIDDEN OUT OF TOWN ON RAIL !!

INDIGNANT CITIZENS TAKE LAW INTO OWN HANDS WHEN FELLOW-TOWNSMAN REFUSES TO CO-OPERATE IN BEAUTIFYING TOWN BY WEARING ZOOT-SUIT !!

ZOOT-SUIT YOKUM OFFERED NOMINATION FOR PRESIDENCY IN 1944 !!

THIRD PARTY FORMED, TO BE KNOWN AS "THE ZOOT-SUIT PROGRESSIVES."

ELECTION SEEN CERTAIN !!

THE CONSERVATIVE CLOTHING MANUFACTURERS CALL A MEETING —

IF THIS ZOOT SUIT FEVER CONTINUES UNABATED, WE'LL ALL BE RUINED !!

WE'VE GOT TO FIGURE OUT SOME WAY TO MAKE MEN BUY CONSERVATIVE, SENSIBLE CLOTHES AGAIN !!

GENTLEMEN! —THE IDEA OF "ZOOT-SUIT YOKUM" WAS CREATED BY THE GREAT "IDEA" MAN, J. COLOSSAL McGENIUS, WHO CHARGES $10,000 A WORD FOR ADVICE !! —

IF HE CREATED "ZOOT-SUIT YOKUM" FOR THE ZOOT SUIT MANUFACTURERS, PERHAPS HE CAN FIGURE OUT A WAY OF DESTROYING HIM — FOR US !! IT'LL COST $10,000 A WORD - BUT IT'LL BE WORTH IT !!

MR. McGENIUS, I REPRESENT THE ASSOCIATION OF CONSERVATIVE CLOTHING MANUFACTURERS!

I'M GLAD TO MEET YOU!

(—"HMM !— WOULD 'IT' BE CONSIDERED ONE OR TWO WORDS ?-? OH, WELL—I'LL MAKE IT TWO WORDS. THAT'S $60,000, ALREADY!)

ability of children to see faces or grotesque figures in walls, clouds, and so on is very well known. These generally two-dimensional perceptions provide a form of primitive, natural Rorschach test."[28] The popularity of "Zoot-Suit Yokum" yields an unscientific but suggestive notion of the acceptable levels of schizoid behavior in wartime. Schizoid processes signify defenses in which part objects represent whole objects. Thus the predicate "zoot-suit" is symbolically representative of a totality. As developed in Capp's schema, the fusion and condensation of two dissimilar objects take place—at least in the mind of a borderline individual. In Los Angeles this could take the form of "all zoot-suiters are Mexicans" or vice versa. It could also link the image of the zoot-suiter with that of the enemy. Eight days after the last installment of "Zoot-Suit Yokum," the *Los Angeles Times* featured a caricature by Paul Ford in which then Japanese premier Tojo was portrayed as being a "sartorial" dresser, favoring above all a zoot-suit when riding horseback.[29]

Another dynamic approach to understanding the lure of the grotesque in art comes from Ernst Kris and his illustration of the "aesthetic illusion." Kris tenders this vignette from World War II:

> A captain of a Marine detachment on one of the Pacific islands heard from one of the outposts a dim noise of voices. Though the enemy was at safe distance, a gathering of several men required the captain's attention. He approached the spot and found one of his men with a radio set tuned on to an American short-wave station.[30]

The broadcast was about Marines expecting Japanese attacks on their position. Kris poignantly added that "no clear example of 'vicarious participation' is known to me; safety in the aesthetic illusion protects from the danger in reality, even if both dangers should be identical."[31] The aesthetic illusion allows individuals to "indulge in what they otherwise fear."[32] Fantasies of martial prowess, of physically cleansing the country of undesirable elements, and of annihilating zoot-suiters could do much to alleviate ambivalent feelings about war and to assuage moods of dissatisfaction and ennui.

"Art it is said, releases unconscious tensions and 'purges' the soul."[33] In this vein Kris considers the proximity of the Aristotelian notion of catharsis and Freud's use of catharsis as an initial step in therapy. The union that Kris considered to be fundamental for a psychoanalytic rendering of art and its enjoyment was the manner in which catharsis allowed for a discharge of dammed-up instincts and at the same time for their control. Discharge and control therefore afforded a twin pleasure—the pleasure of letting go of repressed hostility and the pleasure of controlling that hostility. Through the preservation of the aesthetic illusion Kris sustained the view that an individual is freed from the strictures of guilt since the release comes from someone else's fantasy.[34] War would certainly heighten the illusion since it rendered the symbolic and actual destruction of the enemy, unpatriotic Americans, and other hate objects socially permissible.

It is difficult to determine the influence of "Zoot-Suit Yokum" on the American public in general and the Los Angeles public in particular any more than official propaganda agencies can be credited with the mobilization or the demoralization of the civilian and military population. An added impediment is that much of the influence of this kind of a comic strip could be unconscious, leaving individuals unaware of the subliminal effect of the message on their psyche. Nevertheless the "Zoot-Suit Yokum" chapter is a gripping precursor of the symbolic developments that typified the riots. The splitting of images into antipodal frames—life/death, patriotism/disloyalty, annihilation/regeneration, innocence/corruption, and hero/villain—anticipated the themes that servicemen and civilians reenacted throughout the Zoot-Suit Riots. There are rites of passage as the conservative clothing manufacturers search for the ideal candidate, initiate him into the status of Zoot-Suit Yokum, then coach him through his ascendancy to the level of popular hero, and then his eventual demise and obliteration. The inversion or reversal of roles, characteristic of transitional ceremonies and seasonal feasts, is seen in the metamorphosis of Abner from the dumbest man in the world to national hero. Likewise Gat Garson, a convicted criminal, goes from Coventry to acclaim as he dupes Abner. Sentiments of homicide, infanticide, and castration run through the cartoon, giving force to Capp's acknowledged preoccupation with death. The power of communal moral indignation reflects solidarity in a time of national crisis. Most of the individuals that appear in the series are marginal actors, briefly achieving notoriety, then resigned to oblivion.

4. Servicemen and Zoot-Suiters

Japan's attack on Pearl Harbor redefined reality for all Americans. Where before there had been a lingering isolationist spirit, a dissociation from things European, the events of 7 December 1941 snapped the mood of uninvolvement and gave notice of national crisis. Social and economic grievances were momentarily deferred. Workers were asked to suspend their claims against management and consent to a no-strike pledge for the war's duration. Young men and women flocked to enlist in the armed forces, while civilians accepted the bleak realities of future anguish, personal loss, and deprivation. There were areas of civil unrest, but for the most part these tensions remained hidden from public view and therefore largely unfelt. The aura of innocence and righteousness was pervasive and even deceived the nominally alert American Civil Liberties Union. So smug was the home front and so united were the citizens in the cause of winning the war that the ACLU found it incumbent upon itself to publish a glowing report on the civility of the home front:

> The striking contrast between the state of civil liberty in the first eighteen months of World War II and World War I offers strong evidence to support the thesis that our democracy can fight even the greatest of all wars and still maintain the essentials of liberty.[1]

The report highlighted the notion that "we experienced no hysteria, no war-inspired mob violence, no pressure for suppressing dissent . . ."[2] The theme of American innocence was endemic and engendered a facade of equanimity that contributed to a self-perpetuating social amnesia.

But there was hysteria. War inspired mob violence and pressure for suppressing dissent. The earliest and most encompassing example was the internment of Japanese and Japanese Americans in the first six months of 1942. The fact that the ACLU report omitted reference to this colossal event suggests that lesser transgressions were similarly repressed in a collective effort to avoid the darkside of the American psyche. As Franco Fornari, a leading psychoanalyst of war, suggested:

> . . . when destructive reality is covered with symbols of love, this may constitute a maneuver destined to conceal deep depressive or persecutory anxieties, and that such concealment is very likely to predispose him who makes it to grave distortions in reality-testing and so render him unable to correctly foresee the possible consequences of his actions.[3]

American propaganda, like that of other warring nations, was designed to promote feelings of omnipotence, righteousness, and the ego ideals that reinforce a semblance of unanimity. Successful propaganda also depended on the constant flow of convincing messages about the Axis threat to the security of the country. The government and military were aware that the public's tolerance for unending war was limited: "General Marshal had made his observation that a democracy cannot fight a seven years' war."[4] Much of the public's dedication to the war depended on its view of the servicemen.

In the gifted hands of John Hersey, Ernie Pyle, and Bill Maudlin, the uncommonly diverse backgrounds of the American fighting men were narrowed to a common denominator. They were typically portrayed as being from the countryside, athletic, highly intelligent (but lowly intellectuals), refreshingly amenable to their temporary subordination to the general will, and always ready to reconvert their energies to peacetime pursuits. "Nice guys, they cared less for Christian friendship than for staying alive, helping their buddies, and getting home to a job, a girl, and a cold Coca-Cola. They were, after all, just like Americans at home."[5] As John Morton Blum added, "There, too, the war could signify on what the culture ordinarily endorsed."[6] Moreover, they were symbolically accessible to the vicarious needs of the public. "The soldiers were not depicted as soldiers, the military; they were civilians in uniform, guys like you and me or our sons and brothers—in short, Us."[7] The propaganda ideal of the citizen-soldier merged with what many Americans wanted to believe about their servicemen. "The battlefields provided a plentitude of such symbols, of genuine heroes who were then ordinarily clothed, whether justly or not, with characteristics long identified with national virtue."[8]

The month of May 1943 was extraordinary in the social history of the American homefront. Widespread jailings, exposés, and a mood of hysteria followed the breaking of the no-strike pledge by John L. Lewis and the coal miners on 1 May. Public reaction spread beyond maligning the striking miners and became increasingly indiscriminate and unrealistic. A headline in the *Los Angeles Times* rekindled the issue of Japanese subversion: "Startling Jap Spy Activity Here Told."[9] A women's group in southern California asked that identity cards be issued to all minors as a safeguard against juvenile delinquency.[10] Also in May came the first nationwide crackdown on draft dodgers by the Federal Bureau of Investigation.[11] The 638 arrests were a painful blow to American propaganda and did little to enhance the reputations of San Francisco and Los Angeles where the greatest number of fugitives were found. An effort to regain some of this lost ground came from the director of civilian defense for the state of California, Williard W. Keith, who suggested the possibility of " 'Face-Saving' Jap Raids" on the west coast.[12] Aware of the growing disaffection and distraction from the wartime priorities, President Roosevelt again in May ordered the dissemination of "stark photos" revealing the physical suffering of American combat men as a reminder to the public of their patriotic and moral responsibilities.[13] As public criticism over rationing, the cost of living, wage controls, and adverse working conditions increased, there was a corresponding decrease in the propaganda value of media exposure to the heroism and sacrifices of men at war. People adapted themselves to news of hardship from the battlefield, but never fully resigned themselves to deprivation at home. The publicly idolized servicemen and privately embittered workers coexisted in relative harmony throughout the war. Although the authorities minimized cases of violence between servicemen and civilians, confrontations were inevitable. In San Francisco the presence of "almost indigestible masses of servicemen" crowding the streets, filling the restaurants, occupying the hotels, clogging an overburdened public transit system, and depleting the availability of liquor led to numerous civilian complaints.[14] To the navy's idea of curtailing shore leave the sailors responded with a sophomoric but telling barb:

> To wonderful San Francisco,
> Liberty town of the West;
> Which provides for its civilians,
> And to hell with all the rest.[15]

By mid 1943 the romance of the ideal serviceman had faded appreciably for both civilians and servicemen. In many instances the psychological behavior of servicemen paralleled that of disgruntled workers, such as the coal miners. There was a notion of "letting off steam"—which in the military took the form of "kidding around"—that exemplified passive resistance to the war. "High priority has been given to such behaviors not only because they tend to develop spontaneously but also because they are likely to provide release from accumulated psychological tensions."[16] Military psychiatrists were particularly concerned with the servicemen's reactions to emotional deprivations:

> There are two major sources of status deprivations which are keenly felt during the first months in the Army. The first is the imposition of certain types of work which have highly negative prestige value in our society. The second arises from the kind of power relations between the private and his superiors.[17]

Sociologist S. Kirson Weinberg identified four major categories of behavior that deviated from the standard military ideal. "Among these types are (1) the 'goldbrick' or 'goof off'; (2) 'the sadsack'; (3) the 'foul-up'; and (4) the 'G.I.' "[18] Weinberg suggested that "some soldiers tolerate the man who shirks petty details, providing he is 'on the ball' in the more relevant activities."[19]

Irving L. Janis, a psychologist working for the army during the war, offered this intriguing class analysis:

> The essential point is that during the first few months in the Army, middle class individuals appear to play the game of goldbricking on routine tasks, unless there is a direct threat of detection and punishment—even when they know that the task is an essential one and that there is nothing to be gained by dawdling.[20]

According to Janis "the essential feature of goldbricking is dissociating oneself from performance of the job by doing as little as one can get away with."[21] Janis further referred to goldbricking as a "game" because the "men seem to 'get a kick out of it.' "[22]

The identification with the sources of power, whether management, union leaders, or the military, is unusually high during periods of extreme stress. One of the more complete statements on this kind of identification comes from Anna Freud and is classically delineated in her concept of the "identification with the aggressor." In her words: "By impersonating the aggressor, assuming his attributes or imitating his aggression, the child transforms himself from the person threatened into the person who makes a threat."[23]

Anna Freud was ostensibly referring to the anxiety experience of children. The same psychodynamics, however, can be seen in the adult or group. For servicemen the identification with the aggressor was encapsulated in the psychology of the GI:

> The "G.I." type who indiscriminately abides by military rules is by no means a variant. On the contrary, he is very devoted to his duties, but often he stresses the more petty rather than the strenuous phases of routine. He may give undue attention to shining shoes, making his bed, cleaning his gun, or being the first one in line or in "falling out." He is ultra-serious in obeying the rules and is the social opposite of the "goldbrick," or "goof-off."[24]

What appeared to the military and the public as a model GI was a distorted response to military duty. The place where servicemen were most likely to undergo this kind of response was basic training camp.

Indeed, apart from combat itself, the most harrowing experience for the enlistee was basic training. Even in retrospect, the celebrated novelist James Jones could not idealize that aspect of the war.

> With the induction ceremony the honeymoon got over pretty quickly. Men who had been raised to believe, however erroneously, in a certain modicum of individual free-thinking were being taught by loud, fat, devoted sergeants to live as numbers, by the numbers. Clothes that did not fit, when they could see clothes on the shelves that did fit. Personal and dedicated harassments over wrinkles in blankets and blemished polishments of shoes and rifle barrels, when it was perfectly clear that neither wrinkle nor blemish existed. Living in herds and schools like steers or fish, where men (suddenly missing deeply the wives or girlfiends they left so adventuresomely two weeks before) literally could not find the privacy to masturbate even in the latrines. Being laughed at, insulted, upbraided, held up to ridicule, and fed like pigs at a trough with absolutely no recourse or rights to uphold their treasured individuality before any parent, lover, teacher or tribune. Harassed to rise at five in the morning, harassed to be in bed at nine-thirty at night.[25]

Men learned to hate the enemy in this fashion and often to make an enemy out of their drill instructors. Basic trainees "dreamed in their sleep nightly, and frequently daydreamed consciously, of killing their 'sadistic' sergeants in cold blood."[26]

The minor but telling disturbances of May 1943 were a preamble to the most disruptive summer of the American home front. Hypersensitive civilians and servicemen vilified each other yet remained relatively controlled in their actions. But in Los Angeles there was one factor that made the imminent possibility of civil unrest more volatile. The key military installations at Terminal Island, the Coast Guard base at Long Beach, the navy compounds at Chavez Ravine, and the operations base at San Pedro, along with the adjoining army facilities at Fort MacArthur were in close proximity to Mexican barrios. This geodemographic layout added a dimension to the conflicts between servicemen and the civilians in Los Angeles. Instead of confrontations between civilians and servicemen, the newspapers recorded clashes between servicemen and zoot-suiters. The press reported every zoot-suiter incident in the California southland, interspersing lulls in activity with special features on the "sociology" of zoot-suiters. The young servicemen, predominantly white, single, in their teens or early twenties, trained for combat, piqued and depressed by the excesses and restraints of military life, enjoyed the immunities of soldiers in a second front—the fight against zoot suiters. Their faults were exceptions, their sins pardonable, and their righteousness monolithic. Few if any noticed that in its severity the zoot-suiters-servicemen rumpus took a back seat to the violence among servicemen themselves and against civilians. In the two weeks preceding the Zoot-Suit Riots, there were eighteen reported incidents involving servicemen in southern California, seven of which resulted in death.[27] The one police action involving zoot-suiters and servicemen during this period was dismissed by the courts for lack of evidence against the arrested Mexicans.[28] There were six incidents of violence between zoot-suiters and civilians with the majority of the civilian victims being Mexicans. In contrast to the fatalities between civilians and servicemen, the conflict between alleged zoot-suiters and draftees remained at the level of taunts and jeers, with scattered sessions deteriorating into brief street scraps. At no time were there any fatalities suffered by either servicemen or zoot-suiters during their fights.

For Los Angelenos who followed press reports on the zoot-suit menace, the seedbed of delinquency was to be found in these young Mexicans who attacked servicemen, skipped induction, and idly cluttered the streets without contributing materially or spiritually to the war effort. Just as journalists, novelists, and propagandists had intensified the public's awareness of the virtues of their citizen-soldiers and recalcitrant workers, a growing literature informed that same public of the vices of zoot-suiters. Where the appeal on behalf of servicemen went to the emotions of empathy, compassion, and brotherhood, the injunctions against zoot-suiters solicited fantasies of revenge, retribution, and annihilation.

The anxieties of wartime generated psychological adaptations that merged so tightly with the distortions of the period as to give neurotic behavior a semblance of patriotic normalcy. It was not uncommon for the worker and serviceman, the young and old, or the government and private enterprise to use the prerogatives of patriotism as a shield for aggression. Yet as the country edged toward internal confrontation, the bitterness and rage was often channeled toward surrogate hate objects. The damage to American propaganda and the morale of the nation from news or rumor of internal social conflict was incalculable. In May 1943 it appeared that the country was on the verge of serious domestic discord.

Strife was hardly new to Los Angeles. Bitter labor, racial, and political disputes dotted the city's history from the time of its colonization by the United States. Conflict had been particularly intense between the Anglo and Mexican communities. In the immediate past there was the notorious and hysterical mass deportation of Mexicans and Mexican Americans. Under the guise of expanding employment opportunities for American citizens during the Great Depression, thousands of Mexicans had been deported in a move that resulted in resentment, bitterness, and no tangible relief from the depression.[29] The removal of Mexicans from California was a godsend to men like Governor Culbert L. Olson, who favored wartime relocation of Japanese to the agricultural fields rather than risk the reimportation of Mexican farm labor. "This would enable California to maintain its important and lucrative agricultural production without importing large numbers of workers undesirable for other reasons, namely, Mexicans and Southern Negroes."[30] Governor Olson's racial preference was seconded by the public idea of a tradition that antedated the unique psychosocial pressures of World War II America.

A barrier to a generalized reaction against Mexicans was that the disruptions that brought loss of status to workers and servicemen also operated in the Mexican barrios. Indeed, the psychosocial transformations of the barrio were a microcosm of the national experience.

While there was a general decrease in adult crime during the war, criminal behavior increased drastically among adolescents. "Juvenile arrests increased 20 percent in 1943; in some cities it was even higher—San Diego, for example, reported an increase of 55 percent among boys and 355 percent among girls."[31] Two reasons for the spiraling rise in delinquency among girls were the war-related surge of prostitution and a concomitant rise in violent behavior.[32] Among boys there was a disproportionate and equally sudden rise in acts of indiscriminate vandalism and violence. In his *Don't You Know There's a War On?* (1976), Richard R. Lingeman gives this phenomenon a psychological interpretation. "Some of these acts seemed a kind of acting-out of war fantasies—such as the thirteen-year-old 'thrill saboteur' who put a stick of dynamite under a railroad track, lit the fuse and ran.''[33] This is remarkably similar to the group behavior of the younger White Fence gang members: "The younger brothers of the Purissima crowd began to call themselves the Commandos and the Pansy Gang. Essentially, they were seen by the neighborhood as kids playing street games. Obviously, these were war games.''[34]

Wartime juvenile delinquency caught the nation unprepared and initially insensitive to adolescent needs. Authoritarian measures against juveniles, delinquent or not, gave way to the emergent culture and power of the "teenager." Teenagers were demographically a majority, legitimate consumers, and the raw bulwark for defeating the enemy. They made demands on society and contributed to the disruption of prewar normalcy: "Social recreation schemes meshed easily with the demand of adolescents to have something of their own. Social centers, glamorized as counterparts to servicemen's 'canteens,' were established in thousands of American communities in the last two years of the war.''[35] Emphasis was clearly on dissipating youthful energy: "dances, swimming parties, jam sessions, table tennis tournaments—every kind of recreation short of sexual intercourse or drinking was encouraged.''[36] It was difficult for adults to see adolescent rebellion as a reaction to the widening realities of an adult world in turmoil. For one, the war imposed adult behavior on young people. Together with the initial adolescent and perhaps even infantile hoopla about making war, combat heroism, and swift victory, there existed the anxiety about leaving home, growing up, adult responsibility, and death. As Redl commented with respect to the zoot-suiter, the whole fad was a means of postponing adulthood. Teenagers relished a separate identity and confronted adults with an unsavory challenge to adult values. The more pessimistic foretold of a generation doomed to lawlessness, violence, and disillusionment; another "lost generation.''[37] Yet in Los Angeles there was a solid distinction between the travails of youth across the country and those of Mexican youth in the city.

In Los Angeles the problem of juvenile delinquency was reduced to a Mexican problem—a zoot-suit pachuco gang-member problem with loose references to drug addiction, promiscuity, draft evasion, and unbridled violence. Even Geoffrey Perrett, who demonstrated his command of this transformation in his *Days of Sadness, Years of Triumph*

(1974), supported the stereotype:

> Zoot suits had meanwhile [by 1943] gone from being the fad of harmless jitterbuggers to being the uniform of young thugs organized in street gangs. Youth dances frequently ended up as free-for-alls. To the standard zoot suit accessories there had been added an ornate switchblade knife for boys and a whiskey flask shaped to fit inside a brassiere for girls.[38]

The conversion of the zoot-suiter into a pachuco was a symbolic simplification. But it simplified a distressing situation and made it symbolically tolerable when juvenile delinquency was presented in terms consonant with traditional self-images, expectations, and biases. The displacement of unwanted feelings was not unusual. However, there was no quantifiable growth in delinquency among Mexican youth in the city. Testimony given before the Los Angeles Grand Jury by the Los Angeles County Probation Department supported, if anything, this conclusion:

> The great majority of Mexican children are not involved in these delinquent activities. As a matter of fact, the total number of Mexican boys brought into Juvenile Court during the first six months of 1943 showed no increase over the number in Court during the corresponding period of last year. An analysis of their cases shows that auto thefts committed by Mexican boys decreased more than the total rate of decrease and that other types of theft committed by Mexican boys increased only 6% (as compared to the 21.8% increase in the total for all racial groups). In other words, there is no "wave of lawlessness" among Mexican children, although there is a specific problem of gang violence that must be, and is being dealt with.[39]

The preceding commentary by Karl Holton went on to warn that "the instances of gang fighting among Mexican youths which have been so well publicized have naturally appealed to the imagination of the public (including suggestible youths who might like to see their names in the papers, too)."[40]

There were, of course, significant problems with Mexican juvenile delinquency. A major source of conflict was the difficulty of entering a new country and culture and adapting to internal and external demands for conformity. Erik Erikson has repeatedly underscored the importance of psychic restructuring, ideological experimentation, and the repudiation of past identities for adolescents. For many young Mexicans these youthful tasks took on added dimensions:

> Undoubtedly the old Mexican custom of giving freedom to adolescent boys is a primary source of trouble. In Mexico a boy of sixteen was ready to assume responsibilities of a family and his life in the community. Here, where both marriage and

employment are deferred, the giving of the same freedom to boys of that age is often disastrous.[41]

By American standards, Mexican youth was deprived of adolescence. While Anglo-American youth voted for their psychosocial status as teenagers with their fads, growing consumerism, and demands for separate entertainment facilities, Mexican youth craved similar treatment: "They ought to erect a statue in the Plaza to the unknown zooter. Cause it wasn't until then . . . until the riots, when a lot of kids got beat up . . . that they gave us our clubs."[42]

Yet even at their most incorrigible, the delinquency of zoot-suiters, Mexican-American youth, and black and white adolescents was never a threat to the stability of the Los Angeles community. If anything, the moral indignation voiced by correctional authorities and public discussion brought about an increased solidarity to the adult population, often at the expense of adolescents. Juvenile delinquency was not an unexpected phenomenon. Adolescent deviancy was an acknowledged part of daily life, at times sanctioned by both law enforcement agencies and the general public. At no time is this more patently demonstrable than during the Zoot-Suit Riots. In fact, the sanctioning of certain forms of deviant behavior is a specific phase of human development. This was accentuated by Kai Erikson in his study on Puritan deviance. An example: ". . . the youth who joins street riots or profanes a sacred ceremony has a kind of permit from his elders to behave in that fashion, and the 'contrary' who obstinately refuses to follow the ordinary conventions of his group is only doing what everyone expects of him anyway."[43]

Tension between servicemen and zoot-suiters was understandably aggravated as much by their dissimilarities as their similarities. Geographic proximity made it impossible for one to avoid the other. The acting-out proclivities of adolescents, whether servicemen or zoot-suiters, dictated much of the behavior between the two groups. Indeed, as Marilyn Domer recognized in her thesis, servicemen, especially trainees, increasingly assumed the behavioral norms of their adversaries, so that the relationship of the servicemen to the zoot-suiters was that of one gang to another: ". . . before long a situation analogous to gang warfare had developed between these two cohesive groups, the Mexican-American gangs and the sailors of the United States Navy."[44] For here were two indigenous cultures, relatively oblivious of each other's raison d'être, imposed upon each other, and compelled to act with a sense of urgency and permanency in a situation that was irrevocably transient. And yet it is unlikely that the buildup of tension between the two adversaries led to the riots. For when the disturbances did occur, they assumed the characteristics of a more amorphous, diffused, and hysterical expression of discontent—a discontent symbolic of a nation undergoing massive psychic upheaval, not one circumscribed to the youthful rumbles of two relatively isolated cohorts.

The symbols of adolescent rebellion seethed throughout the encounters between servicemen and zoot-suiters. Both had uniforms delineating membership in an elite. The zoot suit symbolized youthful disdain for established mores. It was iconoclastic, taunting; a statement of adolescent narcissism, omnipotence, and overcompensation. It conferred entry into a select culture unavailable to servicemen. It represented a state of being popularly perceived as unrestricted and uninhibited. Their clothing, speech, and hairstyle denoted status and group membership and at the same time expressed their individuality. The zoot-suiter also signified a territorial claim where servicemen were unwanted. Theirs was a sanctuary from an older generation, from Mexico, from Anglo America, and certainly from adventuresome servicemen. They projected their status through their cars, clubs, and forms of entertainment. Zoot-suiters had girls, and this became one of the sorest conflicts between them and servicemen. "The Mexican *pachuquitas* were very appealing to American servicemen, and jealously guarded by the Mexican-American boys. They scandalized the adults of the Anglo and Mexican communities alike, with their short, tight skirts, sheer blouses, and built-up hairdos."[45] Indeed, one interpretation of the riots was that they emasculated the zoot-suiters: "The pursuit and beating of zoot-suiters and the destruction of the 'drapes,' or costumes, by mobs of servicemen were so many defeats of Mexican manhood and symbolic conquests or at least the access to the then-undefeated *pachuquitas*."[46] Sexual and racial tensions heightened when southern servicemen were involved. Many transferred southern cultural values to the barrios they frequented. Chester B. Himes, a writer for *The Crises* (a black magazine edited then by Roy Wilkins), reported the behavior of a southern sailor aboard a Los Angeles streetcar as he flirted with a Mexican girl: "When this blond sailor saw her [the young Mexican woman], . . . he began saying in his loud, whiskey-thickened voice, 'Boy, uh white man can git any gal he wants. Can't he boy, can't he git 'em if he wants 'em?' "[47] Added Himes: "And then he went on to elaborate how he fought like a white man, trying all the time to get this Mexican girl's eye."[48] Racial slurring aside, the behavior of this young Anglo sericeman was not unlike the braggadocio of a zoot-suiter. Both took stock in their physical prowess—a commonplace of adolescents.

The similarities between servicemen and zoot-suiters are less obvious yet analytically riveting. The very identity of the zoot-suiter and the basic trainee was ephemeral. Both were members of cultures that by virtue of age and reality represented transient states of being. More often than not, the zoot-suiter would soon undergo the transformation into an inductee. Mexican American youth eagerly anticipated military service, according to the findings of Raúl Morín.[49] The armed forces represented a continuation of barrio fantasies of martial encounters. There was the omnipresent military uniform, its adjunct paraphernalia, a specific linguistic protocol, and a prescribed gait—all of which again denoted status, group membership, and even a form of differentiation from the staid deportment of the civilian. Morín found military life to be the great leveler: "Finding ourselves in a new setting away from the old surroundings, with new faces, and new friends, and everyone in the same boat, put us on equal status."[50] Cultural nationalism tended to fade in the armed forces: "Most impressive was the smooth way that Americans of all nationalities were assimilated in their new life."[51] Meyer H. Maskin and Leon L. Altman, writing in 1943, offered a professional evaluation:

> Army life is group living and cooperation; its goal is a coordinated common effort. The effacement of the self is compensated for by a feeling of participation in an immortal cause. From the tragedy of front-line fighting emerges a mystical and religious faith in the essential goodness of man and the ultimate appearance of a new, free world. The soldier is a crusader and in this exalted role transcends his erstwhile banal preoccupations and life.[52]

In short, military life provided lower-class adolescent males with an escape from the drudgery and limitations of their birthright. And as McWilliams concluded in *North from Mexico*:

> Turning away from home and school, the Mexican boy has only one place where he can find security and status. This is the gang made up of boys exactly like himself, who live in the same neighborhood, and who are going through precisely the same distressing process at precisely the same time.[53]

From membership in the local gang to membership in the armed forces was a historically appropriate advance. Since the 1840s, when Irish immigrants joined the army in the war against Mexico, military service has served the immigrant, the foreigner, and the nonwhite as the fastest way of proving their patriotism.

The relationship, therefore, between zoot-suiters and servicemen was not disparate sociologically, psychologically, or politically. The undeniable distinction was cultural and racial. As Himes recognized, many of the servicemen in the Los Angeles area were from the South, perhaps in intellect and emotion from the Old South. A transference of their phobic, obsessional, and paranoiac reactions to nonwhites, minorities, and "foreigners" was not unpredictable. The integration of the races was a legal and folk belief. Mexicans were nonwhite in parts of the country, and for political and economic reasons officially white in other parts.[54] They were recent deportees who by 1943 were being reimported as an integral part of a great crusade. They were allies in the struggle against the Axis, participating in combat in both the American and Mexican military, yet as implied in the Ayres report, they had more in common with the hated Oriental enemy than they did with the majority of the American citizenry. They were good field workers, but impossible adolescents. The imaginary exploits of zoot-suiters received more news coverage than the combat exploits of Mexican-American medal of honor winners. Sometimes Mexican nationals were favored over their hyphenated brethren in the United States. Still there was a lingering fear that Mexico-based members of the Sinarquistas would infiltrate the barrios and mobilize antiAmerican sentiment. The ambivalence and ambiguity over the identity of Mexicans in the United States was another externalized version of the internal insecurities experienced by citizens in the midst of war.

5. The Zoot-Suit Riots

Wartime exigencies and psychological stress give way to temporary inversions of normal behavior. One could see an anomaly in Communist party support for the no-strike pledge and in its opposition to certain union activities. Official government policy was supportive of the Soviet Union, although states like California continued anti-Communist investigations. One group that went through a variety of transformations in identity, self-esteem, and status was servicemen. While at the start of the war servicemen were uniformly accorded special attention, some of the luster and novelty wore off by 1943. Servicemen themselves were ostensibly less enthusiastic about the war. Rebellious but not unpatriotic soldiers often displaced their feelings of deprivation and death anxiety by maligning the Allies:

> . . . the G.I. "took it out" on "damned Limeys" and "dirty Frogs," but *not* interestingly enough on the Germans and southern Italians who directly gratified his self-esteem by behaving toward him as a conqueror.[1]

However overstated, this formulation by Henry Elkin indicates that the "taking out" of aggressive impulses was not restricted to GI-Allied relationships. In many ways the GI had acquired an identity as hero and antihero.

Although civilian and military authorities cooperated in minimizing violence between civilians and servicemen, confrontations were inevitable. Often the passive aggressiveness of the goldbricker, goof-off, or sad-sack was not enough to contain rage and desperation. Any military training center with a surrounding civilian population could hardly avoid some degree of conflict with servicemen on leaves, on weekend passes, or in transit. This was especially true in areas that offered renowned tourist attractions, such as Los Angeles.

Los Angeles was the temporary home of one of the largest concentrations of military personnel. It was also a choice spot for liberty. On any given weekend during the war up to fifty thousand servicemen from all branches of the armed forces would cram the city to partake of the excitement of Hollywood and the California lifestyle and to simply get away from the drudgery of military confinement. For most of the servicemen these weekends were comparatively innocuous opportunities for a healthy letting off of steam. On 16 May 1943, for instance, over one thousand soldiers training in nearby deserts had been convoyed to Santa Monica for a much-deserved beach party—without incident.[2]

Still, Los Angeles and its environs posed problems and threats to the average servicemen. Among the expected drawbacks of visiting the city were those of being on unfamiliar terrain, with unfamiliar customs, traditions, and peoples. Outstanding among these was the fact that the major military posts were, as noted in chapter 4, bounded by Mexican neighborhoods. Unless the servicemen stationed in these installations had previously lived in select areas of the Southwest or Midwest, they would more than likely have never before been exposed to Mexicans, Hispanics, or the "Spanish." Los Angeles law enforcement officials considered the prevalence of Mexican juvenile delinquency as one of the more ominous threats to the security of the city and, by implication, to that of the servicemen. The most minute item relating to zoot-suiters was an invitation for editorial, sociological, and psychological analysis, debate, and speculation. In contrast there was little effort to explain the growing escalation of violence between servicemen and civilians. The imagery and rhetoric used to stereotype zoot-suiters underscored a widespread level of public discontent.

The zoot-suit menace pales when compared with the violence taking place between civilians and servicemen throughout southern California. Consider the following: Between 1 May 1943 and 6 June 1943 there had been eighteen major incidents involving servicemen, seven of which resulted in death: (1) on 15 May a soldier killed a sailor; (2) on 20 May a sailor was held in the slaying of a civilian; (3) on 21 May a soldier was shot and killed by a civilian; (4) on 25 May a soldier was knifed by a civilian and died later of the wounds: (5) on 25 May a soldier was killed by a civilian; (6) on 29 May a marine was killed by a hit-and-run automobile; and (7) on 30 May two sailors killed a taxicab driver.[3] None of these incidents involved zoot-suiters. Of the incidents not resulting in fatalities, one involved a clash between servicemen and zoot-suiters at a dance in Santa Monica—a case dismissed by the courts for lack of evidence against the arrested zoot-suiters.[4] There were no instances of zoot-suiters killing servicemen. From the preceding it appears that the gravest threat faced by servicemen was the serviceman himself, not the zoot-suiter, and the second most formidable threat was the armed civilian.

For the same period there were seven incidents involving zoot-suiters, one, as mentioned, dealing with servicemen. The balance were confrontations between zoot-suiters and the general population, inclusive of Mexicans. Of these only one case resulted in injury from a stabbing.[5] No one was killed. As the press ran feature stories over the precipitous rise in juvenile delinquency, there was little effort to balance these lurid accounts.

The conflict between servicemen and zoot-suiters was the lowest on the hierarchy of stress-provoking stimuli. It was easier to malign zoot-suiters than to deal with disturbing self-doubts about the course of the war. As Al Capp had shown, the threat to the country was from within. The zoot suit was culturally and aesthetically un-American, at least according to Capp. As a Mexican, the zoot-suiter was identifiably a "foreigner." The desire to rid the country of foreign elements had been accentuated by the war. No doubt there was also a deeply rooted desire to get rid of undesirable or unwanted feelings of ambivalence and hate that ran counter to wartime expressions of loyalty, patriotism, and selflessness. If the Limeys and Frogs could be hated, so could Mexicans. But even here the Mexican was a unique kind of Mexican. It nominally did not mean Mexicans as braceros—for after all they were part of the Allied effort against the Axis. Nor did braceros represent the Mexicans who lived in Mexico. The zoot-suiter was the antithesis of the serviceman, and this, as will be shown later, could evoke the most disparate symbolization.

Previous studies have given the riots a historical place in the pantheon of American racism. Carey McWilliams makes one of the strongest efforts to prove a racist conspiracy against Mexicans. Like Beatrice Griffith, he links the start of the riots to a meeting of Mexican youth (members of the Alpine Club) at a police substation on 3 June 1943—a meeting ironically called by a police captain to discuss the eradication of delinquency:

> After the meeting had adjourned, the boys were taken in squad cars to the street corner nearest the neighborhood in which most of them lived. The squad cars were scarcely out of sight, when the boys were assaulted, not by a rival "gang" or "club," but by hoodlum elements in the neighborhod. Of one thing the boys were sure: their assailants were not of Mexican descent.[6]

In an earlier incident, eleven sailors had allegedly been attacked by Mexicans: "As they were walking along the street, so they later stated, the sailors were set upon by a gang of Mexican boys."[7] McWilliams's point is that the sailors were in fact victims of a police beating:

> When the attack was reported to the nearest substation, the police adopted a curious attitude. Instead of attempting to find and arrest the assailants, fourteen policemen remained at the station after their regular duty was over for the night. Then, under the command of a detective lieutenant, the "Vengeance Squad," as they called themselves, set out "to clean up" the gang that had attacked the sailors. But—miracle of miracles!—when they arrived at the scene of the attack they could find no one to arrest—not a single Mexican—on their favorite charge of "suspicion of assault."[8]

The absence of suspects, according to McWilliams—"so strikingly at variance with what usually happened on raids of this sort—raises an inference that a larger strategy was involved."[9] The function of the police raid, therefore, was to mobilize anti-Mexican feelings and "thus began the so-called 'Zoot-Suit Race Riots' which were to last, in one form or another, for a week in Los Angeles."[10]

Beatrice Griffith also ties the meeting of the Alpine Club with the start of the riots, albeit with significant variations: "The Pachucos from Alpine were meeting upstairs in the Los Angeles Central Jail to organize their club."[11] But unlike McWilliams, Griffith's scourge was against the navy. "It wasn't long until a Mexican-American sailor hollered up from the sidewalk below to two boys sitting in the window. 'You guys better beat it. There's about a hundred sailors hunting for you up at Alpine.' "[12] This marked the start of the riots for Griffith. And, like McWilliams, she envisioned a conspiracy.[13] Up to a week before the 3 June confrontation, sailors from Chavez Ravine and the Harbor area had, according to Griffith, "cased" and "reconnoitered" the Mexican-American community in drawing their "battle map for the riots."

> The sailors walked out of Chavez Ravine Armory armed with rocks, sticks, clubs, belts, heavy weights in their handkerchiefs, and palm saps. They walked out, got into cars and drove over to Alpine. One naval officer later said, "We knew where they were going and the guards looked the other way. Most thought it was high time something was done."[14]

One of the more damning indictments of the servicemen came from San Diego, into which the riots had spread. On 10 June 1943 San Diego city councilman Charles C. Dail, later mayor of the city, addressed

Rear Admiral David W. Bagley, commandant of the Eleventh Naval District in San Diego. Dail's most critical charge:

> The initiative action being taken by soldiers, sailors and marines for the first time directed against the so-called "zoot-suit" wearers is not that alone. It is, speaking for this locality, and has been aimed at civilians in general. There have been numerous instances in San Diego where members of the military forces have insulted and vilified civilians on public streets; and to cite one instance recently: a Consolidated Aircraft Company official, after objecting to the epithets of a marine, pertaining to his civilian status, was attacked and seriously injured and will be unable to return to his duties for some time, as a result of the injuries sustained. Most civilians just "grin and bear it" rather than precipitate an altercation which would be certain if they resisted.[15]

Although Admiral Bagley publicly denied the accusations leveled by Dail, official but classified military memos confirm the councilman's suspicions.[16] Indeed, the most serious wounds of the riots were suffered by a black aircraft worker in Los Angeles at the hands of servicemen.[17]

In the final report on the riots prepared by the navy, in 1951, the elements of conspiracy and culpability are noticeably altered:

> It was on the evening of June 3rd, 1943 that it started. Three young Mexican-Americans met on a dimly-lit corner of the shanty area in which they lived and made plans for their evening's work: rolling servicemen in the back alleys just off Main Street.[18]

After a brief description of their modus operandi, the report continues:

> And it was on this evening that this particular group of enterprisers picked the wrong job. They tackled three servicemen who weren't quite drunk and who knew how to handle themselves. This time, it was the Angelenos who lay on the pavement while the others went their way, refreshed by their "exercise."[19]

The blithe quality of this report is reminiscent of press reports on the riots. Yet the author used restraint in suggesting a "chain reaction" type of explanation for the riots. Thus the beaten Mexican boys gathered some of their cohorts and retaliated against the sailors.

> This act, by the inverted logic of this tense time, required vengeance against the "Pachucos" who had started it, [*sic*] And so it went, until the acts spread throughout most of Los Angeles and caused a hurt that is not totally eradicated even today, eight years later.[20]

And unlike the newspaper reports that banked on sensationalized headlines, this report discounted allegations about the existence of criminally organized zoot-suit gangs.

> What caused all this? The reasons are legion. But there is one reason, despite all beliefs to the contrary, that was not cogent: this was not, in the usual sense of the word, "gang warfare." One of the most important facts of the entire juvenile delinquency problem in Los Angeles was then, as today, the fact that there is *not one gang organized by a single leader for the express purpose of committing crime.*[21] [italics mine]

On 9 June 1943 Admiral Bagley's explanation for the riots was featured in the *Los Angeles Times:* "The official Navy announcement described the sailors as acting on 'self-defense against the rowdy element. . . .' "[22] On the same day of this "official" report, Admiral Bagley issued the following memo to "Activities Los Angeles and San Diego Area, Santa Barbara Advance Base Dept Port Hueneme: The commandant believes that the men now engaging in these demonstrations are actuated *entirely* by a desire for excitement and feels that they have not seriously considered the consequences which may follow from ill considered action" [italics mine].[23] In the copy of the memo on file, the word "entirely" had been scratched out with one line and the word "mainly" was substituted.[24] This memo was directed to Admiral Bagley's commanders and to naval intelligence.

The idea of servicemen "actuated entirely by a desire for excitement" suggests a rebellion against ennui, certainly against the repressed environment of military regimentation. Freud had recognized the symptoms in his "Group Psychology and the Analysis of the Ego" (1921) when he wrote: "We know that the war neuroses which ravaged the German army have been recognized as being a protest of the individual against the part he was expected to play in the army . . ."[25] The dissolution of a group is indicative of the loss of emotional ties. Bombarded by the disintegration of a social order ostensibly dedicated to the unconditional pursuit of winning the war, servicemen became increasingly ambivalent about their own commitments. Griffith was wary of this process:

> But these trainees were away from the usual restraints of home, friends, and work. The war's outcome was doubtful in the summer of 1943. They were eager for a chance to let off steam accumulated for many reasons. They had come from high schools, from behind store counters, and out of factories to be trained for battle. Many were having their last fling before shipping out. This zoot-suit hunt

was a convenient punching bag. Primed by inflammatory newspaper stories, seeking revenge for real and imaginary wrongs, they were here to battle . . . to help their buddies. It was going to be a good weekend in a war-packed city.[26]

At least for ten days in southern California and some adjoining bases, the military lost control of several thousand servicemen. The navy high command appeared to be pleading with the sailors: "The commandant suggests that commanding officers bring the substance of the above memorandum to the attention of the men of their commands in a personal and unofficial manner . . ."[27] The second half of Bagley's "order" was equally passive: ". . . having full confidence that an appeal to the individual based on common sense and reasonableness will invoke prompt response on part of the enlisted men concerned and that they will refrain from such disorders."[28] One of the admiral's subordinates, a captain, suggested a more direct approach: "I have only one suggestion there. You said in the end, 'It is suggested'—I believe it would be better if you ordered every commanding officer to do it."[29]

Military officers in the southern California area were momentarily powerless in their ability to control the "disorderly" bands of servicemen. If they exercised decisive and immediate authority, according to the provisions under the Uniform Code of Military Justice, they would have had to incarcerate and court-martial hundreds and perhaps thousands of servicemen for disorderly conduct, disobeying direct orders, inciting a riot, being AWOL, and, conceivably, mutiny. This would have been an enormous propaganda victory for the Axis who constantly pointed out the internal antagonisms of American society.

The problem of controlling the servicemen was uppermost in the minds of the military authorities. On 8 June 1943, the senior patrol officer in downtown Los Angeles, Commander Clarence Fogg, assessed the "Continued Disorder": "Hundreds of servicemen prowling downtown Los Angeles mostly on foot—disorderly—apparently on prowl for Mexicans."[30] The navy's description of these marauding gangs underscored the severity of the military's loss of authority: "Groups vary in size from 10 to 150 men and scatter immediately when shore patrol approach. Men found carrying hammock clues, belts, knives, and tire irons when searched by patrol after arrest."[31]

On 11 June 1943 Maxwell Murray, major general of the U.S. Army and commander of the Southern California Sector Western Defense Command, issued a memorandum with the heading "*Restricted*

Immediate Action.'' The memo falls short of acknowledging a mutiny:

1 . The recent incidents connected with the so-called "Zoot-Suit" riots involved mob action, and incipient rioting, by many soldiers and other servicemen.

2 . Prompt action to check such action has been taken, charges are being preferred against those arrested for inciting or actually participating in these riots.

3 . It is obvious that many soldiers are not aware of the serious nature of riot charges. Convictions in a recent serious riot have resulted in sentence to death or long confinement.

4 . It is desired that the attention of all Military personnel be called immediately to the critical dangers of any form of rioting and that incidents which may start as thoughtless group action in comparatively trivial offenses or boisterous conduct are liable to develop into mob riots of the serious character. Further, mob rioting usually results in injury to persons in no way connected with initial cause of the disorder. This is true in the case of the recent disorders which resulted in affront and injury of some completely innocent civilians.

5 . Military personnel of all ranks must understand that no form of mob violence or rioting will be tolerated, and that offenses of this nature will result in immediate and drastic disciplinary action.[32]

Both the army and navy were fully cognizant of the extent and nature of the servicemen's behavior. Acknowledgment of "injuries to some completely innocent civilians" implies that both non-zoot-suit-wearing Mexicans and the general public had suffered at the hands of the servicemen.

The overwhelming concern of military and civilian officers was with the control of enlisted men. Unlike the passive resistance of the goldbricker, sad-sack, goof-off, or even AWOL serviceman, the behavior of the rioting soldiers and sailors indicated a breakdown in military discipline. According to one report, the servicemen were emotionally "worked-up":

Yesterday Fogg [senior shore patrol officer] tells me, just to show you how they get worked up, a draft of men came through the station and read about this in the papers and 8 men got out and left; they were supposed to wait at the station for their train, but they started a band and looked for zoot-suiters and started some trouble. The Patrol rounded them up and locked them up but it just shows how excited they get about it from just reading the papers.[33]

The culprit here was the press and its sensationalized coverage of the riots. But the significance of these classified memos is the admission on the part of high-ranking navy and army officers that there was no zoot-suiter threat to the servicemen and that the military had lost control over enlisted men. In attempting to stem the flow of sailors into the city, the shore patrol followed Admiral Bagley's suggestion of "appealing" to "common sense". When two hundred sailors were blocked by the shore patrol "all were disarmed and sent back to their bases or ships with a warning not to return."[34] The largest reported single group of sailors numbered around four hundred.[35] According to the 8 June report by Commander Fogg, "army personnel [were] predominate. . . at the ratio of 4 to 1."[36] In at least one instance a group of sailors was commanded by a confirmed psychotic:

> George Douthit, a sailor, was detained with two others as the leaders of seventy-five servicemen carrying clubs and chasing zoot-suiters. Douthit was an escaped prisoner from the Mare Island Hospital's Psychopathic Ward.[37]

While the military command endeavored to reassert its authority, the riots underwent a metamorphosis. During the first three days of the disturbances, the general public had not been aware of the nature, and perhaps the existence, of the riots. The *Los Angeles Times*, for instance, did not report the riots until 6 June. Until then the riots were very much an affair of servicemen. By 7 June civilians began to join servicemen in chasing, stripping, and occasionally beating zoot-suiters or non-zoot-suit-wearing Mexican Americans and blacks. "On Monday evening, June seventh, thousands of *Angelenos*, in response to twelve hours' advance notice in the press, turned out for a mass lynching."[38] Taxi drivers offered free transportation to the riot areas.[39] Tensions between civilians and servicemen evaporated as the former eagerly defended the actions of the latter: "They rushed into the 'battle' with vigilante eagerness, resenting any sign of police interference with the servicemen."[40] Both civilians and servicemen poured into Los Angeles to join in the riots. "Seven truckloads of sailors came down from the Las Vegas Air Base."[41]

Civilian officials hastened to the support of servicemen. On 9 June the Los Angeles City Council passed a resolution banning the zoot-suit:

> NOW, THEREFORE, BE IT RESOLVED, that the City Council by Resolution find that the wearing of Zoot Suits constitutes a public nuisance and does hereby instruct the City Attorney to prepare an ordinance declaring same a nuisance and prohibit the wearing of Zoot Suits with reet pleats within the city limits of Los Angeles.[42]

Al Capp had anticipated this kind of resolution—another case of life imitating fantasy. Los Angeles police and sheriff officers were reticent in their pursuit of rampaging servicemen. "Indicative of the policy attitude was the comment of one of the local police chiefs, 'You say the cops had a hands-off policy during the riots! Well, we represent public opinion. Many of us were in the First World War, and we're not going to pick on kids in the service.' "[43]

Cases of police negligence in the face of threats to Mexicans and blacks by servicemen laced the ten-day riots. The military felt that the police were incapable of controlling the situation and placed the city off limits beginning on 8 June.[44] Certainly among the more culpable were the newspapers. On one occasion a guideline was printed on how to unfrock the quarry: "Directions were printed for the newcomers on how to 'de-zoot' a boy: 'Grab a zooter. Take off his pants and frock coat and tear them up or burn them. Trim the "Argentine ducktail" that goes with the screwy costume.' "[45] Civilian involvement in the riots reached its height on 7 June when a crowd of around 5,000 gathered in downtown Los Angeles.[46] In testimony offered to the Tenny Committee by a high-ranking police officer the curious allegation that civilians, sometimes Mexican or black, were leading gangs of servicemen arises: ". . . if a group of servicemen were broken up they formed in another place, but always leading each group there was always a civilian, either a Mexican or Negro or white . . ."[47] In another instance reported by the police a Mexican-American serviceman joined with several zoot-suiters in attacking two officers.[48] Los Angeles chief of police C. B. Horall offered this interpretation:

> Another point I would like to make: While there were a great many service men in those crowds and quite a few civilians, and many of those crowds were led from place to place by civilians, not service men, and in some instances those individuals were reported to be of Latin-American extraction.[49]

The police testimony exhausted the list of possible suspects. And indeed, there was ample reason to suspect that Mexicans, like their Anglo and black counterparts, were uncertain about their identity, their status, and their role in the war. However, the Tenny Committee preferred to consider the riots as the work of outside agitators, namely Communist agent provocateurs, while the Communist party blamed Mexican Sinarquistas—both the Tenny Committee and the Communist party taking the identical positions held during the Sleepy Lagoon case.

Conspiratorial theories about civilian duplicity resurfaced as they had earlier. Writing in the *New Masses*, Marion Bachrach was adamant about civilian collaboration with the Axis. Among the alleged conspirators were Herbert Hoover and the Hearst family.[50] The official organ for these conspirators was the Pacific First, an organization branded by Bachrach as "the defend-California-from-invasion boys whose 'military strategy' leads to a negotiated peace."[51] Their goals in the riots: "The Pacific First maneuver was to merge anti-Japanese with anti-Mexican hatred. The Hearst press simultaneously warned of the imminent threat of a Japanese invasion of California and the menace to California citizens of the 'zoot-suit' gangs roving in 'wolf-packs.' "[52] The logic behind this affair was to divert American military forces from Europe, thereby weakening the allied effort against Hitler. In the absence of Japanese in California, Mexicans had been substituted. The Ayres report was used as evidence "for the identification of our Mexican allies with our Japanese enemies."[53]

The question of the origins of the riots was brought up by Mexican consul Alfredo Elias in a telegram to Admiral Bagley:

> . . . I respectfully appeal to you requesting that you take all those measures that you may deem convenient to bring about the cessation of such acts in violation of law and order which have caused intense alarm among my nationals stop this situation the origin [sic] of which remains undefined is presenting inconvenient aspects in the international field and in my desire to maintain by all means the unity achieved up to now between our peoples I beseach [sic] your valuable and effective assistance.[54]

During an off-the-record meeting between Mayor Bowron of Los Angeles, Police Chief Horall, Congressional representatives, the Los Angeles press, the Mexican press, and juvenile delinquent authorities, the Mexican consul explained the riots as being "a juvenile delinquent problem of underprivileged second generation foreigners . . ."[55] There was agreement that no subversive activity was responsible for the riots. But the most pressing concern, according to Captain Heim (who reported the content of the meeting in a telephone conversation to Admiral Bagley), was that the city had been placed off limits: ". . . but, Admiral, what they are hurt about the situation—and oh, how they are hurt—is the city of Los Angeles being placed out of bounds and the publicity they are getting."[56]

6. The Symbols, Imagery, and Rhetoric of the Riots

On 20 June 1943 a riot broke out in Detroit between blacks and whites. When it was over, thirty-four were dead and hundreds lay seriously wounded.[1] Those who escaped from physical injuries were quick to reveal their psychological lacerations as they rushed to purchase rifles, pistols, and shotguns. Similar outbreaks of mass violence occurred in New York; Philadelphia; Evansville, Indiana; Beaumont, Texas; and Klamath Falls, Oregon. Structurally they all bore an initial similarity. They began with a physical confrontation between a member of a group of an ethnic minority and either a law enforcement official or a white citizen(s). Rumors would then spread of retaliation, sexual abuse, and generalized accusations about un-American behavior. Various forms of mob violence followed, in most instances resulting in serious bodily harm to both sides. The Zoot-Suit Riots were unique among the disturbances of the summer of 1943 for they alone came to represent a highly symbolic style of mass protest.

The official and unofficial reports of the riots draw attention to the irresistible urge on the part of the press to give the riots the trappings of a military operation: "Sailors made it a *landing party*, sought out the zoot-suiters in their hangouts, then proceeded with *mopping up operations* . . . " [italics mine].[2] By McWilliams's count, and that of the majority of Los Angeles newspapers, around two hundred sailors from the naval armory at Chavez Ravine had enlisted the services of about twenty taxicabs and proceeded to the center of town, due east, to the principal Mexican-American barrios.[3] This group became known as the Taxicab Brigade. It was also referred to as a "convoy"—a rather passive portrayal—then changed to the more aggressive "task force."[4] The *Los Angeles Examiner* borrowed from the real enemy and unabashedly wrote about the sailors' "blitz."[5] Then in a more conciliatory mood, "blitz" was changed to "punitive task force."[6] Capitalizing on a reprieve in the riots, the *Herald-Express* brazenly proclaimed a lull in the fighting: "Zoot Forces Quiet on Eastern Front."[7] The *Daily News* was less august in its proclamations: "Zoot

Warfare Takes Guerilla Form."[8] Los Angeles city councilman John Baumgartner was somewhere between the "eastern front" and the "guerrilla war" prescriptions: "There is practically a civil war on and the police have got to take more serious action than they have in the past . . ."[9] There was little effort to mollify the acting-out fantasies of the servicemen. Even when they openly declared their criminal intentions, the newspapers approvingly quoted them, often rounding off the quotations in their own embellished imitations of military jargon:

> Shouting, "We'll destroy every zoot suit in Los Angeles County before this is over," the groups of servicemen moved along the sidewalks in *military fashion*—until they spied a zoot-suiter [italics mine].[10]

The perception of the riots as a military exercise had an antithetical corollary. The newspapers alleged a conspiracy on the part of zoot-suiters. In this we see a recapitulation of the fears generated during World War I about German-Mexican collaboration.[11] The *Daily News* was the first to endorse this rumor: "Axis agents have been active in fomenting gang warfare in Los Angeles, it was revealed last night by unimpeachable sources."[12] And on 8 June it continued when the *Daily News* observed: "They [zoot-suiters] are the type of exuberant youth that Hitler found useful. He gave them brown shirts and guns and made their violence legal."[13] The *Examiner* joined the chorus with its own expert witness:

> Two-fisted Rev. Francisco Quintanilla, who was a Captain in Pancho Villa's rebel army, said flatly: "When boys start attacking servicemen it means the enemy is right at home. It means they are being fed vicious propaganda by enemy agents."[14]

The servicemen thus engaged in "landing parties," "mopping up operations," "taxicab brigades," "task forces," "blitzes," "punitive expeditions," "guerrilla warfare," and "civil war," all with the intent of destroying "every zoot suit in Los Angeles County." Yet little happened. There were no mass confrontations or mass killings or woundings; nor was the crazed behavior associated with wild mobs evident. Not unexpectedly, even the *Los Angeles Times* was perplexed by the absence of any serious injuries: "Despite the huge numbers of participants in the rioting, injuries to the youths wearing the pancake hats and ankle-tight trousers were confined to black eyes, bloody noses and bruises."[15] However much they endeavored to exaggerate the "losses" suffered by zoot-suiters, the *Daily News* editorial staff had to settle for a mildly scandalized version of the *Los Angeles Times* report: "Ranks of the zoot-suiters bore many a scar of battle. Aching heads, cut lips, puffy eyes were everywhere in evidence."[16] But aching heads, cut lips, and puffy eyes are not the products of homicidal intentions, nor do they indicate anything approximating a "riot." Given the number and kinds of weapons found on servicemen, what would have been the result if they had actually encountered a zoot-suit gang of the kind portrayed by the press? For example: "The zooters admitted they planned to attack more sailors and would jab broken bottle necks in the faces of their victims, police said. Beating sailors' brains out with hammers and irons was also on the program."[17] According to the *Daily News*, "The zooters attack[ed] only lone sailors, when they [had] the advantage of 30 to 1."[18] Press reports estimated over "100 organized gangs" in the Los Angeles area—these pitted against several thousand battle-trained recruits eager to let off steam.

Marilyn Domer, who carefully and painstakingly computed the reported cases of arrests and hospitalization of injured, concluded that if there was a "riot," it was unique:

> . . . this riot was not much of a race riot in terms of numbers injured and arrested or in terms of general mob behavior. The police officials were near the truth when they described it as a series of isolated fights. Actually only a small number of the general population was involved as either rioters or victims, and there was no general outbreak of lawlessness by the mob.[19]

Nor were those servicemen and civilians that hunted for zoot-suiters very successful: "One conclusion which is evident is that the mobs of servicemen and civilians did not have much success throughout the riot in their hunt for zoot-suiters downtown and even on the east side."[20] From the beginning of the riots the mobs appeared to be more "in an excited holiday mood" than bent on bodily harm or destruction of property.[21] This undoubtedly contributed to the confusion expressed by the military, police, and civilian authorities over who was to blame for the riots. Each accused the other of negligence, while the press focused on zoot-suiter culpability. Los Angeles mayor Fletcher Bowron along with Police Chief C. B. Horall downplayed the confrontations, with the latter taking the position that there were no riots in progress: ". . . some people have chosen to call it riots; I don't think it should be classified as that."[22] Horall was partial to the idea that the general mood was festive rather than hostile: "Quite a few boys had their clothes torn off, but the crowds weren't particularly hard to handle. And the feeling in general among them was one of fun and sport rather than malice."[23] There is reason to suspect that even before the riots, tensions between servicemen and zoot-suiters were abating:[24] "It seems strange on first consideration that the press did not carry the accounts of these difficulties [clashes between servicemen and zoot-suiters prior to the riots] between the sailors and the Mexican-American youth."[25] The elusiveness of the riots led some to imaginative metaphors: District Attorney Fred Howser warned against the continuation of "this sort of Halloween violence."[26]

Racist imagery permeated the riots and Carey McWilliams, Beatrice Griffith, Eleanor Roosevelt, the Mexican consulate, and even the navy report of 1951 and some of the navy reports of 1943 contended that the riots had been motivated and fanned by Anglo racism. Chester Himes and others mentioned the presence of southern whites as a contributing factor.[27] The overwhelming fact that those chased and beaten were for the most part either Mexican Americans or blacks is a graphic elaboration of the phobic fears of dark-skinned peoples harbored by whites. *Time* magazine endeavored to place the riots in the context of the long history of racism in California: "And Los Angeles, apparently unaware that it was spawning the ugliest brand of riot action since the coolie race riots of the 1870s, gave its tacit approval."[28] Civilian and military law enforcement authorities agreed that the press had been irresponsible in encouraging racial animosities via a sensationalized inflammatory editorial and journalistic style. If nothing else, racism diminished the international posture of the Allied cause and politically undermined American claims of egalitarianism. A widespread popular and academic belief held that the riots had been the work of Mexican Sinarquistas: "It is stranger still that the recent 'zoot-suit riots' between Mexicans and United States Navy men should occur in Los Angeles, the Sinarquist stronghold in this country."[29] This rumor was tied to Axis Fifth Columnist activities in the United States as well as Latin America and, as shown in chapter 2, would be one of the arguments used by the Communist party to explain the riots. Notwithstanding a thorough probe of Mexican-American neighborhoods in Los Angeles and other cities in California by the Federal Bureau of Investigation that failed to yield any evidence of Sinarquista plots, rumors persisted about the infiltration of barrio youth by foreign agents. We see in these thoughts about Mexican Americans a condensation of disparate symbols. There were, for example, the Mexican-American youths who, by virtue of their genetic make-up and cultural heritage, were disposed toward violence and sinister behavior and who were fundamentally unreliable. Then there were the passive, easily led Mexican Americans who were highly vulnerable to the machinations of the Axis. Leonard Pitt recognized this pervasive ambivalence as a characteristic of Anglo-Mexican relations in California:

> The Mexican-American discovers that "Anglos" are far less kindly disposed toward the living Mexican Americans than toward the imaginary Californios and he claims that Yankees fawn over the clay caballeros sold on Olvera Street [Mexican tourist attraction in Los Angeles] but tend to show contempt for the people who sell them.[30]

These contradictory perceptions of Mexican Americans were poignantly displayed throughout the riots. On 4 June, one day after the riots had begun, a cable from the U.S. naval attaché in Mexico City to Admiral Bagley noted the reaction of Mexican naval personnel and their wives during a six month period in which Mexican naval vessels had undergone "repairs and outfitting operations."[31] The naval attaché considered the visit to California by these sailors and their families a diplomatic triumph: "The Naval Attaché feels that the excellent impression gained by this Mexican personnel is of valuable assistance in furthering the good will which exists between the United States and Mexican Navies."[32] These, too, were the sentiments of the American vice-consul at Manzanillo: ". . . it is believed that the majority of their crews will now prove to be good will ambassadors in furthering better American and Mexican relations."[33] Responding on 12 June to the naval attaché, Bagley bordered on condensation:

> In Addition to the official relationship as outlined, personal acquaintances and associations with representatives so gracious of manner and typical of Mexican Citizenry was most pleasant to all District Personnel concerned and experience for future enjoyment.[34]

Since exchanges were classified restricted, whatever propaganda value derived either for Mexican-United States relations or the Allied cause was consigned to secrecy. Given the energetic effort on the part of the Axis to mobilize anti-American feelings in Latin America, it was essential that counter-propaganda be widespread and effective. The American vice-consul at Manzanillo was aware of this need: "This exchange of ideas [between Mexican naval personnel and both American and Mexican Americans in California] evidently proved to be most stimulating to these Mexican citizens and did a lot to help better their opinion of the United States."[35]

There was a general effort by civic officials in Los Angeles to dispel the opinion that the riots had been "race riots." The Los Angeles County Grand Jury was adamant in rejecting racist motives in the course of the riots: "Ill-informed and reckless persons, by unfounded charges of racial discrimination against the Mexican people, have done little to promote harmony between this nation and our sister republic to the south."[36] Yet others, like the members of Governor Earl Warren's Citizens' Committee, which investigated the riots, concluded that ". . . the existence of race prejudice cannot be ignored."[37] Los Angeles County sheriff Eugene Biscailuz and Preston Hotchkiss, a prominent member of the state Chamber of Commerce, agreed that the riots had not been racial in nature.[38] Among the views aimed at defusing talk of racism was the notion that the riots involved zoot-suiters, who were not, after all, representative of the Mexican-American community. This thesis went against Ayres's genetic biological generalizations, which melded the zoot-suiter with the whole of Mexican history. There was, as several students of the period have suggested, a "conditioned" approach toward Mexican Americans and Mexicans. As Arturo Madrid-Barela put it:

> Already conditioned by the centuries-old heritage of anti-Spanish, anti-Catholic sentiment, by the century long campaign of vilification and violence against Mexicans, and enmeshed in the xenophobic and racist atmosphere of World War II Anglo America easily accepted as justifiable the most recent of attacks on its Mexicans. Whatever the Pachucos may have been historically and despite the efforts of an objective portion of the press and populace to place them in a proper historical context as the alienated and brutalized products of a racist and exploitative society, the vision that Anglo America and many of America's Mexicans came to have of the Pachucos was that provided by the press and the police: Namely that they were biologically inferior, culturally degenerate, criminally inclined, sexually promiscuous, bloodthirsty, drug-addicted, etc.[39]

Yet at times even ardent defenders of the status quo, such as Los Angeles Police Chief Horall and county sheriff Biscailuz felt the "riots" were nothing more than routine disturbances.

The elusive quality of the riots is demonstrated by the profound discrepancies between the words used to describe the events and the events themselves. As seen earlier, the servicemen's rhetoric was that of a pseudomilitary maneuver aimed at the annihilation of zoot-suiters. The press reported battles, skirmishes, assaults, etc., and showed that only about one hundred individuals were hurt seriously enough to warrant medical treatment.[40] Civic leaders were at odds over whether "riots" had indeed taken place. Tangible evidence associated with that of destructive mob violence was mysteriously absent from police and military records. Official and popular sentiment was similarly divided over whether the riots had even been racial confrontations, although this was something of a tautology since racism was as de facto in California as in the rest of the United States in 1943. Still the uneasiness revealed during the riots—an uneasiness that was atypical of, for instance, law enforcement agencies during the Sleepy Lagoon trial—underscored a deep ambivalence among Mexicans, servicemen, the press, and the police and sheriff departments.

Psychological analyses were abundant. The focus was on the behavior of Mexican-American youth. Ayres, Redl, Bogardus, Domer, even Governor Warren's Citizen's Committee clearly emphasized the psychology of being a zoot-suiter, the impact of stress on the impoverished and discriminated communities, and personality factors that led to an "inferiority complex."[41] The stigma of pathology was placed on the zoot-suiter and stretched to include political and cultural deficiencies in the Mexican-American community. It was even placed, at times, on Mexican history itself. The obverse reaction was to historically isolate the zoot-suiter and reduce Mexican-American youth to a marginal equation that was neither Mexican nor American but merely an entity subject to the correctional procedures of social workers and law enforcement agencies.

Clearly, there was a problem of juvenile delinquency both within and without the Mexican-American community during the war. But during the riots, zoot-suiters were never involved as *principals*, either in attacking servicemen or civilians nor in being attacked, stripped, or otherwise engaged in any significant physical contact. "One conclusion which is evident is that the mobs of servicemen and civilians did not have much success throughout the riot in their hunt for zoot-suiters downtown and even on the east side."[42] Indeed, "most of them [zoot-suiters] had no quarrel with the sailors to begin with."[43]

The discrepancies in the perceptions of the various witnesses during the riots give added credibility to Leonard Pitt's idea about a "schizoid heritage." Yet Pitt was being descriptive and properly demurred from making any psychodynamic interpretations about the processes of individual and group behavior. Yet there was a deluge of emotional extremes. These distortions often paralleled older and more popularly held beliefs. It was therefore possible for McWilliams, Griffith, and others to argue that the riots were the result of a long tradition of racism against Mexicans in California. Much of the primitive scapegoating behavior of the servicemen seemed identical to that seen during earlier periods of mass racism, nativism, and xenophobia. And, indeed, racism was a factor in the riots. But this ordinary line of thinking begged an enormously sophisticated assumption, for it implied that these young recruits, unaware or indifferent of the existence of Mexican Americans prior to military induction and training in California, were capable of divining historical antecedents and were politically conscious of their action. The opposite was suggested by well-intentioned champions of the zoot-suiters who perceived separatism, revolutionary spontaneity, and cultural nationalism, where in reality there was an adolescent fad and generational rebellion. In both cases adolescents and young adults were credited with behavioral norms well beyond their intellectual and emotional capacities.

These rioting servicemen were not, for the most part, ambulatory psychotics rampaging through a defenseless city. Their behavior pointed to a mass reaction that assumed a symbolic and relatively festive mood. Photographs show servicemen and civilians, men, women, and children, cavorting with each other, their faces tamed by the absence of danger, milling around a stripped zoot-suiter, whose tattered clothing gave proof of the mob's limited intentions. The threats that were leveled against zoot-suiters were sandwiched between self-imposed restrictions that represented the most disciplined side of the servicemen's initiative. There was no looting, burning, raping, or killing. What transpired was a carnival-like atmosphere in which servicemen and civilians acted out inhibitions about the war in a complex series of symbolic rituals of death, rebirth, initiation, and role reversal.

The salient characteristic of the servicemen who left their posts on 3 June in pursuit of zoot-suiters was that they did so in the spirit and manner of the very gangs they intended to annihilate. By the reckoning of their superior officers, these servicemen were "disorderly" and loosely organized into "groups" or "bands." More likely they were organized into gangs and exhibited the indecorum, lack of discipline, and disorderliness of civilians—indeed, of civilian adolescents. In this respect these servicemen were retreating from their imminent status as warriors to their earlier status as adolescents and civilians. At the same time that they resorted to preinduction ways, they conjointly upgraded their military status by taking on many of the behavioral traits of their drill instructors. The markedly juvenile pantomime of playing soldier as expressed in the Taxicab Brigade and other pseudomilitary formations was a mockery of military discipline. Recruits were leaving their posts without authorization and often against direct orders. Yet once out in the civilian world they pretended to be engaged in a military exercise. And while the public, coaxed by the press, clamored for the physical annihilation of the zoot-suiters, servicemen restricted their homicidal activities to symbolic ceremonies in which they cornered their quarry and gave him a military haircut, afterward proceeding to "unpants" him: "As police and shore patrolmen rushed to the scene the servicemen would disperse, but only after they had 'unpantsed' the wearer of the comical clothing."[44] At times the police would join in the ritual: "Police and servicemen cruised Brooklyn Avenue, beat the boys from Maravilla unmercifully, cut their long ducktail hair, and stripped off their clothing when possible."[45] On one occasion the police saved several young braceros who were seemingly unaware of the travesty of their fashion:

> Four Mexican nationals imported to Santa Ana for agricultural work and apparently unaware of the annoyance their trick garb and haircuts caused among servicemen were given police escort to their homes when surrounded by the "commandos" and said they planned to get haircuts immediately.[46]

The majority of the servicemen participating in the riots were recruits and far from jelling into "commandos." They were still at that stage, as Irving Janis observed, in which recruits might try to sever their ties to the civilian world by deliberately disrupting civilian order.[47] Sociologist Henry Elkin noted that hostile impulses toward civilians by servicemen were higher during periods of being off duty:

> So, as soon as he found himself "off-duty" or otherwise beyond the scope of rules and regulations, the soldier characteristically felt supremely "free" and sought to release his impulses and feelings. This release was especially marked in everyday speech and conversation, and its distinguishing feature was a general rebelliousness, expressed in various shades of negativism, from mildly cynical humor to scathing denunciation.[48]

A corollary to the off-duty syndrome was the manner in which servicemen used their time off to continue their passive resistance against military discipline. When they stripped and gave a haircut to the zoot-suiters, they were not degrading Mexican youth as much as they were aggressively mimicking and reenacting their own experience in basic training. Through the "stripping" rituals of basic training, these recruits had lost their identities as civilians and in-dividuals. This loss had come about in the most unceremonious and ignominious manner as groups were hauled into depersonalized lines where each was swiftly given a haircut, "unpantsed," and put into the drab nondescript garb of the recruit's uniform. Basic training was a symbolically castrating experience, a death initiation rite, in which the reborn adolescent would emerge as a warrior in the tradi-tion of his predecessors. But prior to graduation the recruit had to endure a potential break with reality. A postwar study by Peter Bourne brought out the emotional hazards of the induction and training rituals: ". . . The experience does seem to represent in many ways a personal disaster, with the first 24 hours being equiva-lent to the period of the catastrophe in civilian situation."[49] Bourne also recorded a corresponding somatic abnormality:

> . . . investigators have found that it [basic training] is reflected quite dramatical-ly in the 17-hydroxycorticosteroid levels in persons in this situation. These levels are comparable to those seen in schizophrenic patients in incipient psychosis and exceed the levels noted in other supposedly stressful situations.[50]

Of the many indignities suffered by the recruit, Bourne marked two as being uniquely ego damaging: "Particularly meaningful for the late adolescent are the loss of personal clothing and the shaving of his hair."[51] Bourne labeled the early stages of basic training as a "series of stripping processes."[52]

The stripping and haircutting of zoot-suiters resembles a degrada-tion ceremony in which recruits took the role of drill instructors and zoot-suiters were assigned the part of the recruits.[53] In their role of drill instructors the recruits transformed and reconstituted the identity of the zoot-suiters through a series of denunciations and the physical destruction of the artifacts that gave symbolic meaning to their iden-tity—their hair and clothing. Popular civilian and military sentiment endorsed these performances and considered them to signify the dissolution of the zoot-suit menace.

One fascinating aspect of these rituals is the unconscious material that surfaced alongside the stated purpose of the riots. In his classic *Primitive Rebels* (1959), E. J. Hobsbawn gave high regard to the emotional side of mass demonstrations:

> Demonstrations, whose original purpose in labour movements was utili-tarian—to demonstrate the massed strength of the workers to their adver-

saries, and to encourage their supporters by demonstrating it, became ceremonies of solidarity whose value, for many participants, lies as much in the experience of "one-ness" as in any practical object they may seek to achieve.[54]

The moral indignation expressed during the riots served to enhance the ideal of national solidarity—an ideal taxed by strikes, wage freezes, extended working hours, rising absenteeism, goldbricking, and, most of all, increased tension between the civilian and military communities. The riots momentarily met the multiple needs of a population in transition, uncertain as to the future and fraught with premonitory anxiety. Through the mass regression seen during the riots, public notice was given that the initiatory rituals that had transformed the nation from a peacetime to a wartime society were psychologically insufficient for the task of maintaining the illusion of homefront solidarity. The effort to involve the citizenry in preparations and activities that would reaffirm their commitment to the unconditional surrender of the Axis was dampened by the geographic and often emotional distance of the battlefront. The Office of Civil Defense had been charged with maintaining the homefront. There was a limit, however, to the symbolic efficacy of "practice blackouts, . . . air raid alarms and coastal patrols."[55] Even the "volunteer guerrilla units", civilians playing soldier, would have to be disbanded."[56]

By mid 1943 the profound physical and emotional discontinuities of wartime had factionalized many citizens. As important as the social dislocation suffered by the majority of Americans during the war was the psychological disorientation that accompanied often sudden and unpredictable change. Young recruits had an ambiguous identity as potential warriors and potential casualties. Workers enjoyed full employment, but wondered about reconversion to peacetime and the then expected depression that would follow. Families were separated as children went into the armed forces and breadwinners relocated in different parts of the country. Traditional values and beliefs, folk or otherwise, were overturned by wartime exigencies. Women and minorities worked side by side in predominantly white male preserves. The teenager, as a cohort with newfound purchasing power and as a force in consumer tastes, was just emerging. New kinds of crime, inclusive of the black market and sophisticated white-collar variations, were paired with renewed warnings about juvenile delinquency, drug addiction, and incontinence. The impact of these gnawing changes was not stressful enough to give birth to mass popular delusions about an apocalypse. Nor was the gathering momentum of public discontent reason enough to panic the nation's leadership into a Thermidorian reaction. The public was caught between a descending anxiety over the prospect of losing the war and an ascending anxiety over the prospect of enduring further deprivations in the name of bogus patriotism.

War, one would suppose, is ego dystonic. The boundaries of normal behavior are distorted, primitive fantasies are suddenly sanctioned by society, thoughts of killing and revenge receive popular endorsement, and self-effacement rather than self-aggrandizement becomes idealized and often codified into daily life. War alters perceptions of inner and outer reality and forces individuals and groups into the extremes of emotional regression and philosophical speculation. War offers the promise, somewhat ironically, of new beginnings, new experiences, and new horizons. Suicides diminish during wartime, presumably on account of a heightened interest in the future.[57] There is always the promise of redemption, rejuvenation, and revitalization. War is akin to a spiritual revival. It engenders ritual purification and, among modern civilizations, it ensures a demographic cleansing of surplus populations.[58]

War also evokes the ultimate experience and imagery of annihilation. Death is pervasive. Even here there are differing gradations of what Robert Jay Lifton calls "psychic numbing."[59] The massive experience of death is internalized by the living. Object ties, relationships, intimacy, all become problematic and potentially hazardous. As Eric Leed showed in his study on World War I, the combat survivor inherits a set of experiences that is inherently uncommunicable save to another survivor.[60]

No nation can endure the enormity of psychological and physical deprivation without a measure of ambivalence, self-doubt, and indecision. The propaganda allegories of the enemy were having a decidedly ineffectual impact on the American public by 1943:

> As the initial wave of patriotic emotion passed, as sacrifices became more demanding, as the danger of invasion disappeared and victory grew more certain, people became more likely to look out for themselves. The longer the war lasted, the more the balance shifted from public and collective to private and personal concerns.[61]

As a temporary condition in the service of defeating the Axis, civilians and servicemen were willing to undergo the deprivations and humiliations of wartime exigencies. Yet as the general public returned to the quest for prewar aspirations, servicemen, particularly the returning combat veterans were quick to assail their civilian counterparts. "To the overseas men who returned—the wounded, injured, sick—perhaps nothing was quite the slap in the face as the vast and sanguine confidence of the home 'front' after mid-1943.''[62] More volatile still was the servicemen's complaint over wartime profiteering:

> Another thing that shocked, and even rankled, was the richness of everybody. True, we overseas men had read all about it in the home papers that got up to us, but even the hyperbole of newsprint had not done it justice. True that the thirties had been lean years, and that everybody was belaboring it for all they were worth. Who could blame anybody for making everything he could out of such a good thing? (After all, who knew how long it would last?) But the sheer magnitude of it shocked. And there were moments when it seemed they were truly making it off our red meat and bones.[63]

City councilman Charles Dail had tried to warn Admiral Bagley of the growing rift between servicemen and civilians:

> Every civilian, no matter what type of clothing he is wearing, should be safe on the streets, and it is certainly the belief of the writer that the superior officers of servicemen should vigorously discourage any adverse attitude that they may have to civilians, cautioning the personnel that every civilian is not a "draft dodger" and a "slacker," and that a great majority of such civilians in this industrial area are engaged in the building of vital war materials.[64]

The identities of both civilians and servicemen were in a state of flux. Workers had been initiated into the defense industry or defense-related employment. They had sacrificed wages, hourly schedules, their personal comfort, and often their careers for their country. Servicemen had likewise undergone a ritualized entry into the military, had forsaken the status and pleasure of civilian life, and were about to take the next step into combat or combat-related activity, from which they could return intact, in part, or not at all.

To view these pivotal transitions as simply conditioned responses to crisis behavior would be to deprive them of their richness and pageantry. This brings to mind an observation by the philosopher Mircea Eliade: ". . . initiation is so closely linked to the mode of being of human existence that a considerable number of modern man's acts and gestures continue to repeat initiatory scenarios.''[65] Like much that happens in the unconscious and preconscious, these events remain inaccessible for the vast majority. Furthermore, writes Eliade,

". . . every human existence is formed by a series of ordeals, by repeated experience of 'death' and 'resurrection.' And this is why, in a religious perspective, existence is established by initiation; it could almost be said that, insofar as human existence is fulfilled, it is itself initiation."[66]

Life lacked the promise of future fulfillment during the war years. But eventually the excitement, novelty, and even innocence of making war gave way to a frustrating ambivalence. For many there was neither death nor resurrection but an ongoing undefined middle ground. The pioneering anthropologist Arnold van Gennap reduced the question of individual and group change to a series of symbolic passages divided into three general categories: (1) rites of separation, (2) rites of transition, and (3) rites of incorporation.[67] Victor Turner advanced van Gennap's schema by elaborating on the qualities of the ritual process in primitive and modern societies. It is Turner's contribution to an understanding of this middle ground, of the transitional period in any initiatory scenario, that most concerns this section. Turner's concept of liminality, introduced in chapter 2, serves to illustrate the meaning of symbolic and physical transitions of, in this case, servicemen and civilians. *Limen*—indicating "threshold" in Latin—is extended by Turner to include the "characteristics of the ritual passage" as the individual "passes through a cultural realm that has few or none of the attributes of the past or coming state."[68] Leed sees the liminal state as "closely analogous to the position of men in war."[69] There is a fitting quote by Leed of Turner's definition of liminality as a "stripping process":

> Victor Turner asserts that the symbols that characterize the liminal initiand are most often those of effacement or ambiguity: They are often considered to be dark, invisible like a planet in eclipse . . . ; they are stripped of names and clothing, smeared with the common earth and rendered indistinguishable from animals.[70]

In addition, "liminal beings . . . have no status, property, insignia, secular clothing indicating rank or role, position in kinship system—in short, nothing that may distinguish them from their fellow neophytes or initiands."[71] Ironically, it could be argued that the zoot-suiter, liminal that he was, represented a member who had achieved ritual incorporation into a group. He possessed a secret language, practiced precise customs, and had a defined identity. Zoot-suiters represented the antithesis of the patriotic GI, and at the same time embodied qualities that evoked a primitive attraction and idealization: "The heart of the zoot-suiter's way of life was jitterbugging, it provided a kind of orgiastic release for pent-up energies. Zoot-suiters played hard, drank a lot, fought over girls, crashed parties and broke them up by starting fights, and sometimes engaged in criminal activities."[72]

One of the more engrossing liminal experiences is seen in *rituals of status reversal*. These rituals may be cyclical and are

> usually of a collective kind, in which, at certain culturally defined points in the seasonal cycle, groups or categories of persons who habitually occupy low status positions in the social structure are positively enjoined to exercise ritual authority over their superiors.[73]

As Turner noted, the process of role reversal is closely tied to that of the "identification with the aggressor" defense as defined by Anna Freud.[74] Both views see this transformation as an effort to identify with the sources of power by taking on their characteristics, therein neutralizing a threatening object or, in fact, replacing it. Rituals of role reversal permeated the Zoot-Suit Riots. Servicemen assumed the characteristics of cadre or combat veterans in their pantomime of military maneuvers. Instead of being simple recruits they advanced to leaders of "taxicab brigades," executed "flanking movements," "guerrilla warfare," etc., against the enemy. They marched in quasimilitary formations, policing each other as their drill instructors previously had, while forcing captured zoot-suiters to undergo the ritual humiliation and degradation of losing their hair and clothing. There was also a reversal from an identity signifying orderliness and discipline to that of the zoot-suiter. Like the zoot-suiters, the rioting servicemen allegedly played hard, drank, fought over girls, crashed parties, theaters, and neighborhoods, started fights, and some engaged in criminal activity. Finally, the servicemen reverted to their former status as civilians and adolescents in refusing to recognize the authority of the military police and shore patrol, by their refusal to return to their posts, and in their mockery of things military.

Civilians, at first hesitant over the course of the servicemen's behavior, joined the melee on 7 June. They pretended to be servicemen and mixed with groups of recruits as they organized and carried out their zoot-suit hunt. Civilians exhorted the servicemen and both united in a common purpose. City journalists and press photographers pretended to be in combat and embellished their accounts with grotesque imitations of mortal struggle. Civilian officials often sanctioned the servicemen's behavior by downplaying its significance, by direct encouragement, or by the haphazard enforcement of legal statutes prohibiting mob violence.

At a moment when the possibility of violent confrontations between servicemen and workers seemed imminent, the animosities between the two receded, the past was forgiven, and a renewed sense of fraternity among the antagonists emerged—however fragile and momentary—in the place of adversity. Role reversal in this context meant more than just a politically symbolic form of passive resistance. It also meant a shared moral indignation that served to reintegrate two increasingly alienated entities: ". . . anthropologists generally agree that. . . reversals, like other rites and ceremonies of reversal, are ultimately sources of order and stability in a hierarchical society."[75] Where some historians are uncomfortable with the idea of the meaning of the crowd, anthropologists consider certain kinds of crowd behavior, especially those in which role reversal occurs, to be in the service of tradition: ". . . they do not question the basic order of the society itself. They can renew the system, but they cannot change it."[76]

The general absence of violence and destruction of private and public property and the "festive" atmosphere that typified the riots at their height suggest there was no conscious intention to change the establishment or social order. The "achievement" of the rioting servicemen and civilians was a renewed sense of camaraderie, solidarity, and national purpose. Yet there was a political price for their behavior. Military authorities recognized they had lost control of their men. As General Murray warned, the behavior engaged in by servicemen was treasonable and punishable by death. Servicemen who refused to obey direct orders were not contributing to the stability of the armed forces. There was the question of propaganda—not necessarily that of Axis propaganda, but rather the impact of this kind of knowledge among servicemen of diverse ethnic backgrounds. Raúl Morín notes that Mexican-American servicemen were held responsible for the alleged activities of zoot-suiters.[77] Finally, there was the impact of the riots on the national mind—an event that seemingly authorized the start of rioting across the country.

In a restricted psychological and geographic sense, the riots contributed to the reintegration of two nominally antagonistic groups at the expense of the third group. The relatively small group of servicemen and civilians who participated in the riots had resolved their grievances. There was no more talk of mass strikes, absenteeism, goldbricking, goofing-off, or being AWOL. The riots encompassed all of the forms of letting off steam. Participants were acting with apparent impunity from legal or moral sanctions. Civilians and servicemen had come together and joined in a spirited union. There was spontaneity, a pervading sense of oneness, a feeling of regeneration, of freedom from the strictures of wartime. While there had been an increased distancing between civilians and servicemen, the riots restored an earlier intimacy and gave notice that both shared a profound communal bond. Not since the early days of the war had such excitement flourished in Los Angeles.

7. "The Hard to Get At"

The navy command in Los Angeles and southern California drew contingency plans aimed at preempting a recurrence of the June confrontations. The navy was certainly pressured by the need to maintain a stalwart propaganda effort free of the embarrassing and potentially damaging repercussions of having enlisted men running amok. Yet the navy had trouble coming to a definitive conclusion on the origin and nature of the Zoot-Suit Riots. Instead, it focused its concerns on what the future could hold and shifted its energies to a reassessment of the "Negro problem."[1]

The navy may have taken a cue from the Detroit riots of 20 to 21 June 1943, in which twenty-seven blacks and seven whites were killed. The navy was recognizably the most segregated of the armed forces. There was undoubtedly some comfort in the support it received from civilian law enforcement agencies. A report to *Comeleven* (Commandant Eleventh Naval District) by Commander Clarence Fogg, senior patrol officer in Los Angeles, underscored the sentiments of the Los Angeles Police Department: "(b) The Chief of Police and his assistants reported arrests of members of the negro race had increased nearly 100% compared with a year ago."[2] One measure of the deviance attributed to blacks was the rise in venereal disease. Perhaps it was not so much the high incidence of venereal disease that bothered the authorities, but the fact that it also reflected interracial contact: "Further . . .the armed forces complained of a high incidence of venereal disease, and reported that many of the contacts were made in the Central Avenue Area, involving black and white prostitutes, directed by negro panderers."[3]

Law enforcement authorities struggled to make sense of the conditions plaguing the city's minorities. With the support of Mayor Bowron and "various and unofficial sources," the navy gathered some thoughts on the problems afflicting the black community.[4] There was agreement on the existence of discrimination; lack of transportation, recreation, and housing; and police brutality. Commander Fogg gave the reasons for these developments:

> (g) An immigrant increase to the local negro population at the rate of about 1000 per month, mostly from the Shreveport, Louisiana Area, where racial conditions were bad. This being complicated by similar conditions existing in Los Angeles, resulted in a let down and increase of crime and lawlessness.[5]

The theory was that depressed socioeconomic conditions indicated imminent rioting by blacks. Yet blacks did not engage in any sustained pattern of crime against the Anglo community. The navy also had several assessments about black servicemen.

With respect to "colored personnel": "it appears that racial disturbances on public carriers may originate with colored Army personnel, and become the initial responsibility of the Military Police."[6] The army and navy dutifully recorded instances of conflict with black servicemen. Both services were adamant about vigorously controlling "disorderly colored service personnel inclined to riot: . . . the Shore Patrol teamed with the Army Military Policeman, will necessarily be injected into any disorderly situation that arises. It is submitted that disorderly colored service personnel, inclined to riot, will not have the same respect for a night stick as for a pistol."[7]

These reports were dated 29 July 1943, and on 31 July the navy announced an ambitious plan for retaliation. It proposed three "waves" of attack against the expected black rioters. The plan called for a united effort between Marine Corps, army, and Coast Guard personnel stationed at Terminal Island under navy command.[8] In October 1943, Commander Fogg reassessed the black menace:

> The existing local racial situation grows more tense. It appears to spring directly from an aggressive campaign sponsored by local, state and national representatives of the negro race. Apparently this campaign is founded upon a planned policy of agitation designed to promote unrest and dis-satisfaction among the local negro population.[9]

Fogg's thinking derived from his experience during the Zoot-Suit Riots:

> The Senior Patrol Officer is concerned regarding the number of attacks being perpetrated by negro hoodlums on service personnel. It is assumed that to some extent the cause is related to the incitement conditions described above. However, if continued, retalliation [*sic*] by service personnel will be provoked, with resultant participation in rioting and racial disturbances as per the recent "Zoot-Suit" rioting.[10]

Commander Fogg was certain "that a racial out-break in Los Angeles could occur at any moment and without fore-warning."[11]

Given responsibility for maintaining military order, the shore patrol under Commander Fogg was trusted with resolving the conflict between civilians and servicemen, and specifically between blacks and sailors. But the navy, less so than civilians, was unprepared to deal with the complex issues of immigration, integration, and adolescent rebellion. Its principle concern was in providing combat efficiency. In proposing the creation of an antiriot unit, armed with lethal weapons, the navy may have also reacted to the Detroit riots and further aggravated racial tensions.

Civilian authorities likewise struggled with the meaning of social disorder. One of the more ambitious efforts came from the Joint Fact-Finding Committee on Un-American Activities in California, chaired by state senator Jack B. Tenny, also known as the Tenny Committee. This committee undertook to investigate both the Sleepy Lagoon Defense Committee and the Zoot-Suit Riots. The Tenny Committee had preconceptions about the most serious threat facing the internal security of the country, and reported that the Communist party was a greater danger than Axis Fifth Columnists. In the Sleepy Lagoon case "the Communist Party had a new cause celebre."[12] The Citizens Committee for the Defense of Mexican-American Youth was perceived as "the most prominent of the new agit-prop [agitation propaganda] committees" fronting for the Communist party.[13] The Tenny Committee explicitly absolved the Axis from any form of involvement in the political activities surrounding the Sleepy Lagoon trial. In testimony before the committee on 23 June 1943, Clyde Shoemaker, a member of the Los Angeles County district attorney's office who had participated in prosecuting the Sleepy Lagoon defendants, noted there had been a thorough investigation of possible foreign infiltration of the Mexican-American community:

> . . .I'm satisfied—in fact, I think there is no doubt about it—that there is no Axis influence in the case whatsoever, or any of the cases, never the slightest evidence of any efforts by any of the Axis powers or any of the agents of the Axis powers to incite any of these people to commit any of these deprivations. We never found any evidence at all in that direction.[14]

When it came to Communists, Shoemaker was similarly unequivocal:

> But this group of radicals, whatever you call them—now, when you call them Communists, I want to refer to them as our own breed of Communists, I don't blame Russia—and I don't want to confuse our Communists with those people, that is, they are only a breed, whether you call them Socialists or Socialist radicals or Socialist revolutionaries, they speak a language which in the courtroom always sounds the same. They attack the law enforcement, they put the policemen on trial. . .[15]

Shoemaker's distinction between different "breeds" of Communists was part of a convention that had racial and social undertones. We see this again in his testimony concerning the support by "the better elements in the Mexican community" of the prosecution of the Sleepy Lagoon defendants: "On the other hand, we found that probably the group, the hoodlums that made up these gangs, an aggregate of some 300 out of the total Mexican colony of nearly 300,000, we found the better elements in the Mexican community, the respectable people, all the law-abiding Mexican citizens, heartily approved our prosecution."[16]

The Tenny Committee shied away from investigating allegations about the judicial impropriety of Judge Charles Fricke or the questionable tactics of the prosecution. Yet even after the verdict against the defendants was reversed on 4 October 1944 by the Second District Court of Appeals, the Tenny Committee maintained its contention that the various Sleepy Lagoon defense organizations were covert Communist party fronts.

Implied in the committee's tenacious belief that the Communist party had infiltrated the Mexican-American community was the assumption that Mexicans were incapable of politically organizing themselves, and therefore their mobilization was of necessity attributable to outside agencies. This kind of thinking made it difficult for any politically active Mexican American not to be associated with Communism. Even nonpolitical but presumably extralegal activities, such as the alleged role of Mexican-American youth in the Zoot-Suit Riots, was explicable in terms of Communist infiltration. Hence this view of the riots:

> The *Pachuco* or so-called "zoot-suit" fad among Negro and Mexican youth in Los Angeles' east side was a golden opportunity for Communist racial agitation. The riots that occurred in June of 1943, together with the activities of certain Communist front organizations and the vociferous charges of the Communist press, forcefully brought the situation to the attention of the Committee.[17]

Had it not been for the Communists, therefore, Mexicans would have remained oblivious of racial discrimination: ". . . in accentuation, stimulation and furtherance of the 'class struggle,' the Mexicans of southern California were to be impressed with their 'minority status.' "[18] When Al Waxman, editor of the *Eastside Journal,* a small local newspaper, charged that the major newspapers had sensationalized the issue of Mexican-American juvenile delinquency, the committee defended the metropolitan press and in turn accused Waxman of, in fact, being an agent provocateur. The testimony relating to Waxman is of interest for it revealed another dimension of the committee's collective mind. It shifted the source of conflict from zoot-suiters and servicemen to zoot-suiters and Jews in the Hollenbeck area. Waxman was portrayed as a Communist party operant.

Carey McWilliams, himself the focus of intense cross-examination by the Tenny Committee, was behind the creation of another investigative committee. In his words: "I chaired a meeting of a hundred or more citizens at which an emergency committee was formed to bring about, if possible, a return to sanity in Los Angeles."[19] One result of the meeting was to persuade Governor Earl Warren to form a Citizens Committee to investigate the origin of the riots. Governor Warren appointed California attorney general Robert Kenny to head the Citizens Committee:

> The committee immediately assembled in Los Angeles where Mr. Kenny presented to them a proposed report, with findings and recommendations, which I had prepared at his request. With some modifications, this report was adopted by the committee and submitted to the governor. Out of the work of our emergency committee there finally emerged after a year of negotiations the present-day Council of Civic Unity.[20]

The Citizens Committee concluded there was racial prejudice, police harrassment and brutality, and a lack of housing, employment, and recreation facilities, but almost completely left out an assessment of the role played by Anglo civilians and servicemen in the riots. Governor Warren, however, agreed that not all Mexicans were zoot-suiters, but that the origin of the riots stemmed from the presence of juvenile delinquency.

Beatrice Griffith wrote that the committee "was the determining factor in the riots' end."[21] This seems unlikely since the committee failed to take any substantive action throughout the course of the disturbances. The committee did, nevertheless, have a lasting effect on the course of future activities relating to zoot-suiters. As Griffith pointed out, the *Report and Recommendations of the Citizens Committee* "became the basis for later positive civic action when ten youth agencies pushed through a quarter-million dollar Youth Project for Los Angeles to prevent delinquency."[22] This Youth Project became the model for the next decade. Overlapping with this city agency was the California Youth Authority, a statewide program.

The California Youth Authority was considered by many to be one of the more sophisticated in handling juvenile delinquency. Under the directorship of Karl Holton, the Youth Authority boasted a nationally recognized administrator. Holton felt that "small institutions are run for the benefit of the children. . . . Large institutions are run for the benefit of the staff."[23] By early 1944 the agency was overloaded with cases and Holton began looking for new approaches to solving the upsurge in case loads.

At the start of 1944, with the war effort no longer calling for expanding military training facilities, the Youth Authority "entered into a contract with the U.S. Army to operate two camps."[24] According to the agency's own report: "this arrangement proved to be one of the most successful programs undertaken."[25] Similar in some respects to the camps run by the Civilian Conservation Corps, the plan envisioned alleviating delinquency by keeping youth off the streets: "The aims of the program were twofold: (1) to take this group of older boys out of jail and provide decent accommodations and a training program designed to rehabilitate them and (2) to add the labor of 200 to 300 older boys to the war effort."[26] The staff was enthusiastic about the immediate results: ". . . the boys were able to establish themselves as a respected unit in the military family resident in these Army depots."[27]

Unfortunately, the army closed the camps due to a declining need and the agency was unable to continue funding the operation. Holton's initiative generated another alternative when in July 1945, the Youth Authority "entered into an agreement with the Division of Forestry for the establishment of five forestry camps within a radius of 200 miles of Sacramento."[28] The purpose of these camps: "Work projects were planned to tie in with the Division of Forestry postwar improvement and construction plans and Youth Authority wards were used to construct new forestry facilities such as roads and telephone lines."[29] This was a return to the proven methods of the Civilian Conservation Corps—methods not necessarily intended to stem the rise of juvenile delinquency, but rather designed to make the adolescent less visible after the war when authorities expected significant unemployment.

These efforts by the California Youth Authority were progressive and informed by a sensitive approach to the problem of juvenile delinquency. Although the stated purposes of the agency were never explicitly associated with the Zoot-Suit Riots, it may be significant that the California Youth Authority was the result of the Youth Correction Authority Act of 1941, and that the agency "did not begin to function until 1943."[30] In recognition of the sudden increase in juvenile delinquency, a division "called the 'Delinquency Prevention Division,' was established by the Youth Authority in August 1943."[31]

The Los Angeles Youth Project was a scaled-down version of the California Youth Authority. However, Duane Robinson, one of its first directors, quickly acknowledged that "one of the early constructive results of the riots was the development of 'The Los Angeles Youth Project.'"[32] The project had two specific goals:

> The "zoot-suit" riots brought matters to a head. Committees appointed by several governmental units, and by planning agencies like the Welfare council . . . tackled the problems which the riots presented. How to prevent a repetition of such happenings with possibly more serious results was a first consideration. How to deal with the underlying difficulties of which the riots were only the symptoms was a second.[33]

Listed among the first steps taken by the project was the intensification of services in East Los Angeles, downtown, Bunker Hill, Watts, etc., in an effort to "minimize delinquency, replace destructive gang tendencies, and aid youth in their growth into mature American citizenship."[34] The immediate goal was to strengthen the city's "constructive group work" with minority groups. Special targets of the project were both the "predelinquent" and the delinquent. The staff members were concerned with the "hard to get at" youth "who were not interested in the traditional agency programs and whose behavior problems were more vexing than those of the average youth."[35]

Robinson's use of the word "vexing" to designate the class of youth who defied classification suggests some of the difficulties encountered by the project. There was an overemphasis on administrative specialization and a gaping lack of knowledge and understanding about zoot-suiters. The staff functioned best when it was organized into work-study committees, reorganizing boards, joint agency programs, recruitment and training groups, and special units and when it tried experimental procedures. These sophisticated formulae had limited application to the practical work of eradicating a gang structure that, in fact, did not exist. However, like much of the behavior of servicemen, civilians, and zoot-suiters themselves, the bureaucratic activities of the project's staff served to enhance a sense of mastery, control, and direction.

"The Youth Project was born out of riots and tension in which delinquent behavior and gangs figure strongly."[36] The belief that delinquency had caused the Zoot-Suit Riots prompted the project to develop a "Special Service Unit" designed to "reach groups of youth who were hard to get at and to work intensively with these groups . . ."[37] In contrast to the typically unglamorous work of youth corrections officers, the project's "work began, in some respects, as high adventure . . ."[38] The concept of a special service unit within a special Youth Project denotes the problem faced in finding the "gangs of youth, who are not ordinarily interested in agency programs and are sometimes delinquent or maladjusted . . ."[39]

While youth authorities tracked the very elusive zoot-suiter, Texan Mexicans were gingerly exploring and nurturing the potential for establishing a heroin market in the Los Angeles barrios. Prior to the war heroin was available in the city but not to an extent that attracted law enforcement surveillance. But the war created an irreversible geopolitical shift in the marketing and control of heroin. The invasion of France and the installation of the Vichy government ended the lucrative connection with Turkish dealers for poppy and likewise destroyed the importation of heroin to the United States via Europe and the Middle East. In its place came the cultivation of the opium poppy in Mexico and the shift to El Paso as the major Mafia import center. "By the end of the war, Mexico had become a major supplier, and the border towns centers of narcotic traffic."[40] When the Texan Mexicans from El Paso expanded the heroin market in Los Angeles their clientele was an ethnically mixed group, with Mexicans making up a minority of the purchasers.[41] Nevertheless, this criminal operation was increasingly aimed at soliciting the business of young people. Neither the California Youth Authority nor the Los Angeles Youth Project were aware of the nature or the implications of hard drug distribution in the California southland.

The postwar period saw another transition in the control of heroin as Tijuana, Mexico, came to rival, then surpass, El Paso. In 1945 the so-called Los Angeles gangs were not significantly involved in drug use. By 1950, the problem of addiction had contributed to an identifiably drug-related gang structure and was serious enough to call for a grand jury indictment and mass arrests by federal agents.[42] By the late 1940s the California Youth Authority had developed to the point of publishing its own professional journal. The *California Youth Authority Quarterly* was meant to "report upon projects and programs of the Youth Authority . . ."[43] But it was not until the Spring of 1952 that a brief introductory article appeared in the *Quarterly* on drug addiction.[44] There were no follow-up articles until the summer of 1957.[45] Almost every other topic from the status of youth in postwar Germany to the retirement minutiae of countless functionaries was faithfully covered by the *Quarterly*.

One of the more intensive studies of the Mexican-American and Mexican populations in Los Angeles was conducted by the Federal Bureau of Investigation between 1943 and 1945. The bureau's efforts focused on the question of subversive activities by either Axis or Sinarquista groups in the barrio; the problem of juvenile delinquency (especially that associated with zoot-suiters); race relations between Mexicans, blacks, and whites; the loyalty of the Mexican community to the United States; the influence of Spanish-language newspapers, magazines, and radio stations; the role of the Catholic church; work habits, places of employment, levels of skilled and unskilled workers, union membership, sources of recreation, and levels of education; and short profiles of political and religious leaders. In addition to Los Angeles, the bureau investigated Kern, Madera, Merced, San Bernardino, San Luis Obispo, Ventura, and Fresno counties and the city of Santa Barbara and its environs. These investigations were an outgrowth of security questions dealing with the Mexican-American community and were undoubtedly influenced by the riots.

The bureau's report was certainly a valiant attempt at making a learned statement about the prevailing social and economic conditions in the Mexican community. In keeping with their modus operandi, the bureau's researchers concealed the identity of its agents, sources, and even the names of authors cited from public materials. The Ayres report, for instance, was mentioned without reference to Ayres. The bureau rebuked his findings: "The theory runs counter to anthropological knowledge. In every cultural group there are some individuals who are born subnormal (not bad), but to make such a claim about Mexican youth as 'Mexican youth' are descended from 'bad' ancestry in general is far-fetched."[46] Furthermore, "some have low intelligence quotients due to their breeding. They are sub-normal, but this does not mean they are 'bad' or that they inherit criminal tendencies as such."[47]

Questions about I.Q. and racial comparisons were uppermost in the minds of the researchers. Test scores in some Los Angeles school districts showed "that the average I.Q. of the Mexican student is 90, compared with 94 for the Negroes and 104 for the whites."[48] However, "contrary to the popular belief" about zoot-suiter delinquency, "the colored race gives teachers and principals the greatest concern."[49] There was a decided bias against blacks:

> There are no California state laws or legal ordinances which discriminate against the Mexicans or impose upon their liberties. The Mexicans, legally and practically speaking, have all the privileges of the theatres, churches, restaurants, transportation facilities, and public utilities, and have not caused the racial problem headaches as have the Negroes.[50]

There were other distinctions between blacks and Mexicans: "Inasmuch as Mexicans have been classified as white by the 1940 National Census, it can be concluded that they come within this code section, and many intermarry with other whites but may not intermarry with Negroes."[51] The 1941 Civil Code of California was explicit about the meaning of "non-white": "The Civil Code of California, 1941, states that all marriages of white persons with Negroes, Mongolians, members of the Malay race, or mulattoes are illegal and void."[52] There was also a tacit recognition of racial differences between Mexicans and Anglo Americans: "The Mexicans tend naturally toward segregation and do not aspire to invade the social and business circles where they are not constantly seen just to test the various degrees of racial tolerance."[53] And there were areas where Mexican Americans and blacks came together: "Some of the gangs in question are jointly composed of Mexican Americans and Negro Americans, although as a rule Mexican-American gangs engage in knife battles with Negro gangs. This joining together represents an interesting development of minority groups that unite with minority groups against the common 'enemies.' "[54] This is a rare instance in which Mexican and black youth were understood in a political context.

For the most part the report downplayed the intensity of juvenile delinquency among Mexican youth. There were allusions to a series of conspiratorial theories—most of them originating with FBI informants. One of them addressed the issue of the Pichukas (which the informant noted stood for pachuco in Spanish), a gang reputed to have been the largest in the city and to have its roots in El Paso. The Pichukas originated in 1935 and presumably engaged in marijuana smoking, felonious violence, and sexual perversions. Alongside these degraded qualities was the alleged strength of the gang since it was a potential conduit for the dissemination of Nazi propaganda and subversion:

> It was often reported that a Mexican from Mexico was the head of the "Pichukas", but his name was never ascertained. Even at this time there were several suggestions that the bands were Nazi controlled and that many of the members might have come from Mexico from the Nazi dominated youth camps. It was recalled that sometime ago a speaker at the "Adventurers Club" had exhibited films, which he had taken in the jungles of Mexico when he and his wife had accidentally stumbled onto one of the concealed airports and landing fields of the Nazis where they had set up a Mexican youth training camp.[55]

These allegations linked Mexican youth with a complicated international conspiracy to overthrow the United States. The imagery of the barbarian Nazis melded with primitive Mexicans in the "jungles of Mexico" was evocative in the same manner as the Ayres report. Another informant preferred the more transparent and pastoral image of the peon: "The Mexican peon class is guided more by what appeals to the sense than by a complicated set of highly rationalized codes. He is a realist and opportunist, enjoying today as much as possible and putting off everything else until 'Manana,' [sic] which may never come. His crimes are usually elemental, simple and overt."[56] The obvious suggestion was that Mexicans were incapable of masterminding the overthrow of the American government. This logic demanded an agent provocateur. Another unidentified informant found the source of trouble in the Sleepy Lagoon Defense Committee: "In this connection, he stated that the agitation caused by the 'Citizens Committee for the Defense of Mexican-American Youth,' commonly called 'The Sleepy Lagoon Defense Committee' had attempted to create antagonism between the Spanish-Mexicans and the local law enforcement."[57] The investigation seemed to move inwardly in concentric circles with each accusation taking the focus off of Mexicans and placing it on Americans themselves. Thus it was not the Japanese,

Nazis, Fascists, Sinarquistas, or even Mexican juvenile delinquents who warranted scrutiny but meddlesome liberal Anglo Americans.

The final conclusions of the FBI report were noticeably less oracular than the assumptions about international intrigue. "Lack of training and education and lack of constructive opportunities account for the offenses committed by the Spanish-Mexicans. In this connection, these individuals are strikingly similar to Americans or any other members of the human race."[58] An informant concluded that "a study of crime among the Spanish-Mexicans 'identifies them as members of the human family.' "[59] We also see this quote from another source: "Not all zoot-suiters are members of gangs—only a small fraction. Not all gangsters are Mexican-Americans—only a small fraction. Not all Mexican-American youths are gang-minded—only a small proportion."[60]

There were two powerful obstacles standing in the way of Mexicans participating in subversive activities. These were the Catholic church and Mexican nationalism:

> . . . the majority of the Mexican people had no use for Fascism or Communism, and he attributed this to the fact that the Mexican population was almost 100 per cent affiliated with the Catholic Church. In view of this fact, he said that the teachings of the Church were diametrically opposed to the teachings of Communism or Fascism, and for this reason alone, the Mexican people had no desire to see such doctrines spread. He also stated that the Mexican people were more or less nationalistic in their beliefs and were quite proud of their country, Mexico, and therefore had no desire to see the growth of any outside organization, such as the Spanish Falange, either in their own country or among their people.[61]

Catholicism and cultural nationalism were the bulwarks of several Chicano activist groups in the 1960s and 1970s—much to the chagrin of the established order. In 1943, it had been the established order that lauded safeguards to assimilation.

Indeed, the report indicated alarm at the implications of assimilation. In the words of an informant:

> He attributed the wave of Pachuco incidents to two things. First, the fact that many of the Mexican youths were drifting away from family and from Church, due to the lack of proper supervision by their parents, and, second, that the large growth in Mexican population and in servicemen in the Los Angeles area, due to the wartime situation, had brought about numerous, spontaneous outbreaks between sevicemen and the Mexican youths. These incidents were in many instances brought about by comments made by the servicemen about the zoot suits being worn by the Mexican Pachucos, which created a great deal of resentment on their part, and in many instances provoked fights and altercations.[62]

A stronger statement was made by another informant: "Mexican parents of Mexican-American boys and girls are baffled by what they term 'this trouble freedom in the United States,' which they find their children adopting—talking back to their parents, staying out late at night, and aping older boys and girls."[63]

The bureau closed its investigation on 12 March 1945, satisfied that there was no subversive activity among the Mexican-American population of Los Angeles or California. In fact, Mexican Americans and Mexican nationals were strongly anti-Communist, and there was some recognition that the turmoil over the wave of juvenile delinquency was a predictable stage in the generational and cultural rebelliousness of immigrants.

By the end of the war the Mexican-American community had been investigated, studied, indexed, and profiled by local, state, and private groups.[64] As Ignacio L. López put it in his introduction to Ruth Tuck's *Not with the Fist* (1946):

> In Los Angeles, out of the guilt of the dominant group, arose a fadism for the Mexican-American. Committees gave birth to litters of other committees. Co-ordinator battled co-ordinator. There was a new set of resolutions every morning. Still, when the emotional fever and the defensiveness subsided, few real gains had been made for or by the Mexican-American group. They were basically where they had been for twenty-five years, and the flare of faddish interest was dying.[65]

The behavior of many of these social control agencies paralleled the symbolic pantomimes of servicemen and civilians at the height of the riots. Although demonstrably less symbolic than the performances of the latter, the collective efforts of bureaucrats, administrators, and field investigators often became ritualistic, ceremonial, and obsessional. These characterological traits served to allay anxiety by engendering a sense of identity, purpose, and direction. Organizational activities deemphasized the emotional content of decision making and reinforced the illusion of distance between self and subject. Most of these agencies viewed Mexicans as remote and possessed of exotic and quaint beliefs, none of which were worthy of taking seriously. Much of the data gathered by these agencies were "soft," grounded on hearsay, gossip, and projection, the latter demonstrated by the navy's reaction to the threat of black attacks. The findings enhanced an atmosphere of control and mastery at a time when events were under the oppressive sway of wartime uncertainty.

Any sane person knew that the enemies were the Axis powers. But the Axis powers were remote enemies whose sharper edges were subdued, exaggerated, and otherwise manipulated by defenders of the Allied cause. The need for a more palpable, immediate, and identifiable enemy was more than a simple matter of scapegoating. The United States was geographically isolated from the war. The vast majority of Americans never experienced as their cohorts in the Pacific and European theaters did—the impact of invasions, bombings, and bombardments. Their experience of the war was indirect, taken from newsreels, magazines, propaganda, and other forms of vicarious participation. The whole nation was engulfed in a culture of war that featured the adoption of warlike rhetoric, thinking, symbols, and identities. In some cases routine administrative tasks were transformed into campaigns against an enemy. Thus a question about juvenile delinquency in a poor Mexican-American neighborhood could end by being a crusade against an internal enemy with international connections to Communism and Fascism. In a similar vein the well-intended Los Angeles Youth Project and the California Youth Authority had donned their field equipment and combed the barrio for zoot-suiter hideouts. Even the shore patrol in southern California, whose normal assignment was to police the relatively innocuous carousals of servicemen on leave, prepared to meet an internal enemy—black servicemen entering or passing through Los Angeles.

Like civilians, workers, and some reporters many of the preceding agencies took on warlike qualities. Their peacetime reputations as prominent and effective organizations often gave way to the pressing urgencies and more flamboyant activities of war-related administrations. The riots had presented them with an opportunity to directly participate in a surrogate war—a home front war where the imagery, rites, and mannerisms of men in battle could be appropriated with impunity.

8. Between Annihilation and Redemption

Infanticide has always been practiced by human beings. Whether through the blatantly savage mass killings of a King Herod or perhaps even the more refined but potentially indiscriminate procedures of a modern abortionist, the termination of human life before maturation is historically commonplace. And although we are well aware of the Oedipal struggle that may lead a child to have murderous feelings toward the parent of the same sex, it is also recognized that infanticidal thoughts and desires are just as commonplace in the unconscious life of some parents. Psychoanalyst Dorothy Bloch has made this subject her specialty.

> The parent's wish to commit infanticide... may be much more prevalent than any of us would like to think and more deadly in its effects than we have any way of calculating. I am not referring to the kind of wish that arises in a momentary fit of rage and is communicated directly in simple terms, but to one which, although rarely expressed openly, is absorbed by the child.[1]

For some the most concrete illustration of this unconscious communication is to be found in the institution of modern warfare. Franco Fornari suggested that "the psychoanalytic knowledge of the unconscious leads us to the discovery of the startling fact that fathers unconsciously desire war in order that their sons may die."[2] And then paraphrasing Gaston Bouthoul, author of *Les Guerres: Elements de Polemologie* (1951), Fornari writes that war is "a voluntary institution, the aim of which is the elimination of young men."[3] Finally, Fornari agrees with Bouthoul that modern war is a form of *deferred infanticide*—the function of which is to eliminate the surplus of young men. It would take a massive scholarly and spiritual offensive to successfully reduce modern warfare to the psychodynamics of unconscious infanticidal wishes. The point here is not to superimpose a psychoanalytic construct on World War II, but rather to ask a question that may have been answered by the Zoot-Suit Riots: Was there an element in the behavior of the servicemen during the riots that indicates an awareness of being either victimized or sacrificed? And if there was, how did it manifest itself?

Like Oedipal conflicts, the Cronus complex (i.e., the parents' wish for the death of offspring) is not manifested in the maniacal deeds of the mentally ill. It is more properly the mental property of the neurotic and safely defended by taboo. Self-deception is subtle and fuses well with accepted folk beliefs about emotional maturation:

> Perhaps the difficulty in tolerating such an abhorrent thought [infanticide] stems from the practice of fitting "parents" and "children" into fixed categories, as though when children become parents they undergo a metamorphosis which obliterates not only their previous condition but all the experiences that characterize it.[4]

There is an obvious continuum between the emotional experiences of the child, adolescent, and adult. It hardly needs to be contended that for many servicemen basic training was an infantilizing ordeal that heightened or revived feelings of dependency, helplessness, and worthlessness. In short, basic training contained regressive features that banked on the ability of a cadre to evoke the least sophisticated and earliest memories of the trainee. The drill instructor assumed the role of a father-mother surrogate whose authority rested on the punitive armamentarium of military protocol. Trainees who resisted the new order in their lives were placed in "foul-up" or "recycle" platoons where they were berated to the point of exhaustion, cooptation, and, finally, conversion. Most trainees succumbed early and accepted the "stripping processes" through which their identities were molded into facsimiles of warriors, tacitly accepting their surrender to a hierarchy of parental-substitutions and at the same time mocking, ridiculing, and symbolically acting out against these authorities. John Knowles in *A Separate Peace* illustrates one aspect of this exchange between Gene and Brinker:

> "It gives me a pain, personally, I'm not any kind of hero, and neither are you. And neither is the old man, and he never was, and I don't care what he says he almost did at Chateau-Thierry."
>
> "He's just trying to keep up with the times. He probably feels left out, being too old this time."
>
> "Left out!" Brinker's eyes lighted up. "Left out!" He and his crowd are responsible for it! And we're going to fight it."[5]

The sense of being set up, offered for sacrifice, perhaps of being dispensable, was largely a subtle and quiet matter. Servicemen did not go around accusing either the public or military of intending to sacrifice them. There were some noticeable exceptions: "Football hero and fighter pilot Tom Harmon returned to Detroit after being shot down in China and told the crowd that turned out to cheer his safe return that they made him ashamed. On their heads he wished the descent of enemy bombs."[6] Obviously this crowd had not realized that Harmon felt as much a victim of the folks back home as he did of enemy action.

The persistence of the wish to "annihilate" during the Zoot-Suit Riots uncovers another dimension of the servicemen's emotional state of mind. The thrust of the servicemen's preoccupation may be found in the repeated symbolic acts of emasculation, castration, and annihilation against zoot-suiters. These rituals were only partially in response to the presence of zoot-suiters—a point that accounts for the relative bloodlessness of the riots. Why then were these intense feelings so rampant and uniform? One answer is that they were induced by the specter of imminent combat with the Axis. But if we consider the possibility that the riots were more damaging to the image of the American command than to the Axis, then the preceding is unsatisfactory. A more plausible answer is that these feelings were a reaction to the infantilizing and symbolically castrating experiences of basic training. The most dramatic illustration of this dynamic was the servicemen's collective attempt to evoke feelings of annihilation, worthlessness, and emasculation in the zoot-suiters just as the training cadre had evoked the same feelings in them. It was infinitely easier to consciously admit that servicemen were retaliating against the alleged abuses perpetuated by zoot-suiters than to grapple with the possibility that the servicemen were doing unto the zoot-suiters what they perceived had been done to them. It is an extraordinary testimony to the servicemen's motives and intentions that of all the options available they chose the ritual of symbolic annihilation as the medium that best conveyed their deepest understanding of surviving basic training.

The theme of annihilation, whether in Capp's cartoon, the servicemen's pledges to "wipe out" all zoot-suiters, or the city's efforts to eradicate gangs, was heightened by the uncertainties of wartime, the diminished capacity of the nation to protect its people from harm, and the general omnipresence of death as the war entered its decisive phase. It was common for some to adopt both the identity of victim and victimizer. The stress of prolonged crisis led many to assume the role of victimizer and search out scapegoats. Robert Jay Lifton gives us an idea of the psychodynamics of this defensive maneuver:

> The advantage of creating a scapegoat is that it allows the survivor group to avoid confronting his own death anxiety and death guilt, to find an absolute resolution to the struggle between internal and external blaming, and to move from victimized to victimizer. A victimizer's image of himself as a victim is crucial. He is likely to feel himself continually vulnerable to the deadly assaults of gods, devils, and enemies, and finds that he can best reassert his life-power by victimizing others.[7]

During the riots the servicemen had identified with the aggressor: In their charade of military prowess they took on the roles of drill instructors, pretended to be combat infantrymen, and issued orders and battle commands to appointed subordinates. The servicemen also mimicked their fathers, who had implicitly called upon them to forsake their identities, risk their lives, and perhaps die on the battlefield. Instead, the servicemen offered other youth for sacrifice. In doing so they had transgressed the military code of conduct and had challenged their superiors to in fact kill them directly. Every time a serviceman refused a direct order to desist from pursuing zoot-suiters, he was inviting the ultimate penalty for insubordination in time of war, that is, death.

The symbolic annihilation of zoot-suiters was a passive demonstration against the authority of the military, in which servicemen restored disparate feelings of depersonalization through identification with aggressor, role reversal, and projecting and displacing their anxieties. The immediate result was the illusion of having renewed bonds of intimacy and camaraderie with civilians and a rekindling of group solidarity.

So intense and pervasive was the imagery of destruction during the riots that it was often difficult for the press, law enforcement officials, and even some of the participants to distinguish between symbolic and physical actions. The predominant view was of several hundred gangs of zoot-suiters unleashed from the barrio and bent on disrupting the life of the city. Within the Mexican-American community a similar view prevailed, except that the threat was perceived in terms of gangs of servicemen (and in some cases policemen) who were randomly roving the streets hunting for zoot-suiters.

Although the attack on the barrio was overwhelmingly symbolic, the sense of having suffered enormous numbers of wounded and killed endured long after the impact of the riots had faded from public and institutional interest. The reason for this may be found in the profound and disturbing realization that the target of the servicemen's onslaught was youth.

The barrio had long experienced waves of racism, xenophobia, and nativism. The massive deportation raids of the 1930s were still freshly etched in the consciousness of adults and youth. There was always discrimination, poverty, and injustice in and out of the community. But never before had the focus of inequity settled so brutally on youth. Every culture tends to pin the promise of a better future on its young. It was no different for Mexican-American families in rural and urban America. The irony was that those who represented the hope for the future were also the most vulnerable. Adolescence is a time of tumultuous emotional and physical growth within which is contained the psychosocial nuclei of adult identity. The seemingly unending disorder of adolescence is a passing phase. It is of crucial importance for the healthy development of the adolescent not to be frozen into a stereotype of perpetual disorderliness. Erik Erikson made this an eloquent appeal:

> Once he is "delinquent," his greatest need and often his only salvation is the refusal on the part of older youths, of advisers, and of judiciary personnel to type him further by pat diagnoses and social judgments which ignore the special dynamic conditions of adolescence. Their greatest service may be the refusal to "confirm" him in his criminality.[8]

One of the significant tragedies of the riots was that they, in fact, "confirmed" the "criminality" of Mexican-American youth—a stigma that was institutionalized by the investigatory activities of youth authorities and law enforcement officials, and that was immortalized in the postwar profile of barrio youth as the quintessential picture of delinquency, marginality, and deviance.

The psychological consequences of this global indictment of future generations of Mexican-American youth are incalculable. They were tainted and bore the onus of a marked group. Indeed, the reign of infanticidal imagery carried well beyond 1943 and contaminated the perception of barrio youth in succeeding generations. Among those who expanded on the deficits of Mexican-American adolescence were both Mexican and Mexican-American writers.

Octavio Paz was an unknown aspiring scholar, heavy with emotional ambivalence for his North American descendants, when he wrote *The Labyrinth of Solitude* (1934). Although Paz wrote mostly of the Mexican national character, he showed equal confidence in describing the nature of Mexican-American youth—particularly pachucos:

> The pachucos are youths, for the most part of Mexican origin, who form gangs in Southern cities; they can be identified by their language and behavior as well as by the clothing they affect. They are instinctive rebels, and North American racism has vented its wrath on them more than once.[9]

Paz, like many before and after him, admitted having difficulty with the term pachuco: "Pachuco, a word of uncertain derivation, saying nothing and saying everything."[10] He was concerned with offering an explanation for the emergence of these young people: "Whether we like it or not, these persons are Mexicans, are one of the extremes at which the Mexican can arrive."[11] Nevertheless, his understanding of Mexican-American youth was qualified:

> What distinguishes them, I think is their furtive, restless air: they act like persons who are wearing disguises, who are afraid of a stranger's look because it could strip them and leave them stark naked. When you talk with them, you observe that their sensibilities are like a pendulum, but a pendulum that has lost its reason and swings violently and erratically back and forth. This spiritual condition, or lack of spirit, has given birth to a type known as the pachuco.[12]

The reference to "stripping" pachucos and leaving them "naked" had a basis in fact and in a tradition first defined by Samuel Ramos, one of Paz's ideological precursors.

In *Profile of Man and Culture in Mexico* (1962 edition), Ramos introduced an early attempt at psychoanalyzing the Mexican psyche. Using a selective Adlerian framework, Ramos sought to account for the Mexican's "inferiority complex": "Others have spoken of the sense of inferiority in our race; but no one, so far as I know, has systematically utilized the concept to explain our character. In this essay a methodical application of Adler's psychological theories to the Mexican is attempted for the first time."[13] Adlerian theory postulates power as the ultimate determinant of human behavior. A fundamental dichotomy instructs all human action. Masculinity, in Adler's schema, means strength, while femininity means weakness. Compensation for a sense of inferiority comes through exaggerated aggression—what Adler termed the masculine reaction or protest—which augurs for power and success. Ramos hypothesized that the Mexican's exaggerated sense of superiority was symptomatic of an inferiority complex.

To illustrate his thesis, Ramos concentrated on the pelado, the ascendant of Mexican Americans as implied by Paz and the lowest rung in Mexico's class system. "The best model for study is the Mexican pelado, for he constitutes the most elemental and clearly defined expression of national character."[14] As an adjective or past participle, pelado literally means "peeled" or "plucked."[15] This is the meaning of "stripping" as used by Paz with reference to pachucos. "The pelado," claimed Ramos, "belongs to a most vile category of social fauna; he is a form of human rubbish from the great city."[16] Furthermore, "since he is, in effect, a being without substance, he tries to fill his void with the only suggestive force accessible to him: that of the male animal."[17] This is the antecedent of Paz's "furtive, restless, disguised" Mexican-American pachuco. This style of thinking is also a class analysis disguised as social analysis, in the case of Paz, and psychoanalysis, in the case of Ramos. As Ramos noted: "He is less than a proletarian in the economic hierarchy, and a primitive man in the intellectual one.[18]

Although Paz later revised some of his views, his reproach of Mexican-American youth was the starting and finishing point for many an inquiry into barrio life. His views rang melodious with Anglo-American prejudices and helped certify the majority position on the marginality and inferiority of Mexican Americans. For Paz the onus was to be placed on Mexican Americans themselves: "He denies both the society from which he originated and that of North America."[19] Paz strongly discounted the significance of racism as a factor affecting the economic and social status of Mexican Americans: "I refuse to believe that physical features are as important as is commonly thought."[20] There was nothing in the cultural, economic, or even genetic makeup of Mexican Americans that accounted for their poignant marginality. But there was a flaw somewhere that eluded Paz but nevertheless had to be disowned. In short, the pachuco zoot-suiter was in no manner an heir of culture but rather an aberration. By disclaiming the implications of this sector of Mexican-American youth, Paz endeavored to restore a more aesthetic and historic ideal of Mexicans, while contributing to the concept of the pachuco zoot-suiter as an ahistorical phenomenon worthy of oblivion.

There was much self-conscious shame and embarrassment in these studies by Ramos and Paz. To a large extent they had internalized a mode of criticism about Mexicans that emphasized marginality, inferiority, and hopelessness. Some Mexican Americans likewise adopted this shaky defense against their own self doubts. One example is that of Manuel Servín, a noted scholar:

> Unfortunately, a minority of the postwar Mexican-Americans, the pachucos or zoot-suiters, reacted in a most un-Mexican manner. Dressed outlandishly, as they followed the styles of less acceptable minorities, they quickly undid the hard-earned reputation of prewar Mexicans. Despite the pious lamentations of social workers, the pachucos in a rat pack manner attacked United States servicemen and, regardless of justification or guilt, gave the Mexican community—which incidentally condemned them as much as the North American—an undeserved reputation for lawlessness, cowardice, and disloyalty. As a result, the heroic service of the Mexican-Americans in the Philippines as well as the outstanding bravery of the proportionately numerous Medal of Honor winners were ignored by the North American whites and blacks.[21]

This concise and passionately written paragraph is an elaboration of all the condemnatory themes raised by the detractors of the pachuco zoot-suiter. Thus, the pachucos were an aberration ("most un-Mexican"); they possessed an uncanny power over events ("undid the hard-earned reputation of prewar Mexicans"); they represented the most vile segment of society ("lawlessness, cowardice, and disloyalty"); and they brought ignominy to the virtue and honor of Mexican Americans ("the heroic service of the Mexican Americans in the [war was] ignored"). The pachuco zoot-suiter had undone the positive image of Mexicans. The only legitimate scholarly recourse was to discredit barrio youth.

The discomfort for these scholars may have been in admitting their own vulnerability to American racism. Servín and Paz, along with other Mexican-American and Mexican authors, dissociated themselves from the realities of barrio life and found sustenance in the imagery of hard-earned reputations and heroic service of prewar and wartime Mexicans. These writers were well intentioned and cannot be faulted for striving to protect and idealize an acceptable image of the "good Mexicans." In this they have much in common with the collective impulse during the war to protect an idealized image of servicemen and the ideal of homefront solidarity at the expense of either Japanese Americans, zoot-suiters, blacks, striking workers, etc.

But perhaps one of the more engaging connections between the riots and the work of Servín and Paz is the continuation, albeit in an intellectualized form, of the imagery of annihilation. Both managed to sever

the connection between zoot-suiters and the cultural identity of Mexicans. As such, zoot-suiters were rendered ahistorical, anomalous,
having no place in the past or future of either Mexico or the United
States. The result was another variation in the theme of annihilation.
Instead of being stripped of their clothing, the zoot-suiter in Servín's
text was stripped of historical identity and significance. Ramos had
performed a similar exercise on the pelado.

The exclusion of a race, ethnic group, nationality, or sex from
history is one of the more complete forms of political and cultural annihilation. Surely Paz and Servín were oblivious of their ideological
kinship with Anglo-American scholars who routinely excluded men-
tion of Mexican Americans in their historical narratives of American
history.

From the start of the confrontations there were groups that defended the legal, political, and social rights of barrio youth. Among the
most enduring efforts was that of Carey McWilliams. McWilliams
was the first to place the pachuco zoot-suit generation within the context of American social history:

> It should be remembered that pachuquismo followed a decade of important
> social change for Mexicans in Los Angeles. During the depression years,
> thousands of Mexicans had been repatriated and those remaining began to ad-
> just to a new mode of existence. The residence of those who had been
> migratory workers tended to become stabilized, for residence was a condition
> to obtain relief. Thousands of Mexicans were replaced, during these same
> years, by so-called Okies and Arkies in the migratory labor movement. A
> greater stability of residence implied more regular schooling, better oppor-
> tunities to explore the intricacies of urban life, and above all, it created a situa-
> tion in which the Mexican communities began to impinge on the larger Anglo-
> American community.[22]

McWilliams likewise addressed the unique history of Mexican immigration, the inherent difficulties in obtaining proper education, the
status of Mexicans in labor organizations, the effect of racism on
assimilation, etc. But among his more intemperate descriptions was
that of Anglos during the riots. "On Monday evening, June seventh,
thousands of *Angelenos* in response to twelve hours' advance notice in
the press, turned out for a mass lynching."[23] The imagery of "mass
lynchings" has obvious historical roots in the South. McWilliams's
condemnation was totalistic and inflammatory: "Street cars were
halted while Mexicans, and some Filipinos and Negroes, were jerked
out of their seats, pushed into the streets, and beaten with sadistic

frenzy.''[24] One of the more saccharine passages concerned the plight of Mexican mothers and families: ''Scores of Mexican mothers were trying to locate their youngsters and several hundred Mexicans milled around each of the police stations and the Central Jail trying to get word of missing members of their families.''[25]

Moses Rischin, social and immigration historian, concluded: ''Even Carey McWilliams, who popularized the cause of the nation's minorities in a series of books based on the California scene, came up with a truncated story, for his concerns were too immediately programmatic and his historical research too perfunctory to allow for depth or balance.''[26] While the range and sensitivity of McWilliams's work laid the cornerstone for Mexican-American history for at least two decades, he tended to overexplain and overdefend highly politicized and transitory aspects of the Mexican-American experience. His exemplary but inextricably myopic defense of pachucos forced him to accept the short-term gains of political expediency. Even at his most refined and ideologically precise moments, McWilliams was susceptible to hyperbole and could define the Zoot-Suit Riots as a police plot against Mexican youth. The theme of institutionalized conspiracies circulated among both the defenders and detractors of the pachuco zoot-suiters.

Another variant of the Paz thesis is that the pachuco zoot-suiter was the first to deliberately resist assimilation: ''The purpose of his grotesque dandyism and anarchic behavior is not so much to point out the injustice and incapacity of a society that has failed to assimilate him as it is to demonstrate his personal will to remain different.''[27] Here Octavio Romano ties pachuco resistance to assimilation to the political consciousness of the Chicano movement of the 1960s and 1970s. This interpretation achieved national popularity following Luis Valdéz's celebrated play ''Zoot-Suit.''

Although Valdéz acknowledged the fictionalized nature of his plot and characters, he too attempted to legitimate the historical place of the pachuco zoot-suiter as political activist:

> Pachuco determination and pride grew through the 50's and gave impetus to the Chicano movement of the 1960's. In 1955, shortly before he was stabbed to death in Phoenix, my cousin Billy talked to me about *Chicanoism.* By then the political consciousness stirred by the 1943 zoot-suit riots had devolved into a movement that would soon issue the Chicano Manifesto—a detailed platform of political activism.
>
>   But the first in this direction had been taken by the pachuco, for he was the first Mexican-American to take pride in the complexity of his origins, and to resist conformity.[28]

These two paragraphs represent the continuation of a mythologized zoot-suiter either cast in the role of a descendant of Aztec primitivism or ennobled by a set of modernized attributes. They also represent the primacy of fantasy over reality. The play "Zoot-Suit" can be seen as a ceremonial and festive ritual in which the status of the pachuco zoot-suiter was restored and elevated. The focus of "Zoot-Suit" is on the Sleepy Lagoon trial. The trial is presented as a mockery of judicial procedure. There is a mockery within a mockery as the trial itself becomes the subject of mockery in the play. In a reversal of Al Capp's rendering of zoot-suiters as grotesque, moronic, and savage beings, "Zoot-Suit" shows the prosecuting lawyers, the judge, and the press as members of a bizarre, insensitive, inquisitorial, and thoroughly unscrupulous gang. They are hopelessly oblivious to the subtleties and richness of Mexican culture and, particularly, to the complexities of life in the barrio and the experiences of Mexican-American youth. The pachuco in turn is shown as a heroic "existential" force that helped shape a new identity for Mexican Americans and will continue to "enlighten members of the larger community." This fascinating reversal also witnessed widespread support for the saga of zoot-suiters from the Anglo-American community. Indeed, the play itself would have been financially impossible without the ardent support of Anglo backers.

Yet perhaps the most ironic twist was the fact that "Zoot-Suit" recreated an image among both the Anglo and Mexican-American communities of barrio youth as inextricable from the pachuco experience. Luis Valdéz wrote about having the right "climate" for a play that would appeal to a general audience. This notion suggests a psychological predisposition, a suggestibility, that would allow the public at large to accept the symbols, facts, and fictions about zoot-suiters as positive. Another way of phrasing this is that all that was reprehensible, forbidden, and threatening about the zoot-suiter was no longer a political issue. It was also important to consider the fact that the zoot-suiter, however much anathema to the consciousness of Anglos and Mexican Americans, was a remote, quaint, and putatively harmless archetype endowed with extraordinary powers. We repeatedly learn more about the character of the friends and opponents of zoot-suiters than about zoot-suiters themselves.

A more recent version of the escapades of zoot-suiters comes from Thomas Sánchez, who, in his *Zoot-Suit Murders* (1978), brings together an imaginative cast in which an undercover agent attempts to vindicate a group of zoot-suiters accused of murdering two FBI agents by exposing the un-American activities of Mexican Sinarquistas who had infiltrated the gangs.[29] This plot reintroduces the thesis of Mexican-American complicity with the Axis on the home front and extends the alleged treachery to Mexican nationals. And once again the zoot-suiters are featured as unwitting participants in complicated murder mysteries in which they are finally exonerated.

In the preceding we see two general interpretations of the riots from the Mexican and Mexican-American communities. The Paz/Serviń thesis disowned the zoot-suiter and found refuge in what is often called *lo mexicano*—the accepted context within which appropriate and inappropriate cultural behavior is determined. It reasserted the inviolability of the "true" Mexican identity and spared the authors from having to account for the zoot-suiters. The implication is that they were the product of assimilation and may also represent the negative aspects of American culture. This conservative interpretation of the riots, like those presented by the Tenny Committee and the Los Angeles Police Department, perceived the disruption as an aberration, perhaps not so much because of the primitive origins of the zoot-suiters but because they fell outside of the bona fide Mexican-American experience. Likewise, therefore, the riots are trivialized and rendered outside the scope of legitimate scholarly interest by Mexican and Mexican-American authors. Thus the riots were dissociated from the mainstream of history and isolated from serious scrutiny. Another implication is that the representatives of this school could not tolerate the stressful ambiguities presented by the riots: to admit to weaknesses and failures within the Mexican-American community was an overwhelming indictment of national and ethnic identity. Indeed, it was not unlike the difficulty of tolerating dissent in the home front during the war.

But neither can the other view, that the riots were a racist and perhaps conspiratorial attack on the barrio, be dismissed because of faulty evidence or self-serving bias. It is, in fact, one of the singular realities of the event. It hardly needs to be said that historical "truth" is not the stuff of political or emotional identity. Why, then, would Mexican Americans derive sustenance from perceiving themselves as victims?

The question of victimization emerged in various guises throughout the war. An early instance was the pleasure taken by Los Angelenos from the shared fantasy of having been raided by Japanese airplanes in

February 1942. The romance of victimization in these instances differs from simple masochism in that the latter centers on pleasure derived from degradation, humiliation, and injury. The benefits gained from celebrating these largely symbolic defeats belongs to a higher order of organization. For Mexican-American scholars, writers, and the general community, the perception of the riots as an unprovoked racist attack by marauding sailors was not the product of a collective delusion. Rather, it was consistent with the impulse to order, structure, and define an experience that was otherwise irreducibly chaotic, fragmented, and emotionally unassimilable. Just like civilians and servicemen had fashioned a series of explanations that made sense of the disconcerting extremes of wartime, the Mexican-American response to the riots was to place them within an eminently recognizable context. Whatever the inherent contradictions in the theses presented by Carey McWilliams, Luis Valdéz, or Octavio Romano, they represent a response to the riots that was and to an extent continues to be culturally appropriate. Here, too, the irrational element was attributed to outside forces. And like most of the thinking that characterized the reaction of the collective Anglo community, Mexican Americans developed theories that ranged from simple formulations about the racist motives of the servicemen to more complicated allegations of a conspiratorial nature. The romance of victimization was a group defense mechanism that reiterated the historically recognized vulnerability of the community to racist, xenophobic, and nativist attack.

The foremost function of this response was that it simplified what otherwise could be a bewildering set of disparate emotions, experiences, and contradictory messages. Mexican Americans had been invited to participate as equals in fighting the Axis—and indeed, a legacy of ethnic pride in distinguished military service was born out of the war. Mexican nationals were likewise asked to join the crusade by working in the Bracero Program, thereby releasing American citizens for defense-related work or for combat. Still, racism remained a de facto reality for Mexicans in the United States. The Zoot-Suit Riots removed the ambiguity for some and furthered the distortion for others.

Perhaps the most enduring distortion is the riots themselves. The pervasive belief that riots are indicative of the massive psychosocial disintegration, destruction of property, and mayhem that, for instance, typified the Detroit Riot of 1943 prevails and has been indiscriminately applied to the Zoot-Suit Riots. Where usually we see attacks on barrios and ghettos as forms of unbridled scapegoating, paranoid projections, and undisguised hostility, the Zoot-Suit Riots were exceptional for they served to conceal rather than abreact the irrational and atavistic side of the mob.

Appendix A

8 June 1943, Memo from Commander Clarence Fogg to the District Patrol Officer

0045, June 8, 1943

The following message for information to the District
Patrol Officer.

Dictated by Senior Patrol Officer downtown Los Angeles.

Quote:

Continued disorder.

Hundreds of service men prowling downtown Los Angeles
mostly on foot - disorderly - apparently on prowl for
Mexicans.

Have by joint agreement with Army Provost Marshall
declared following Los Angeles city territory out of
bounds to all Navy-Marines, Coast Guard, and Army
personnel. - Main Street east to Los Angeles city
limits.

All shore patrol are concentrated in the downtown area.
Disorderly personnel are being arrested by shore patrol.
Expect adverse publicity in morning newspaper.

Los Angeles Police have called in all off-duty men and
auxiliary police to handle situation.

Naval Reserve Armory did not grant liberty. Men involved
are from Marine activities, San Diego and El Toro, Navy
activity composed of Roosevelt Base, Port Hueneme , and
Destroyer Base, San Diego.

Situation under control at present except for widely
separated incidents.

Groups vary in size from 10 to 150 men and scatter
immediately when shore patrol approach. Men found
carrying hammock clues, belts, knives, and tire irons
when searched by patrol after arrest.

Army personnel are predominate tonight at the ration of
4 or 5 to 1.

Senior Patrol Office will call District Patrol Officer at about 1000 today, June 8, 1943, if there is anything additional to report.

Given by R. O. Smith, C.M.M.   COMMANDER FOGG.
Received by Halbut.

Appendix B

9 June 1943, Memo from Comeleven to "Activities Los Angeles and San Diego area, Santa Barbara Advance Base Depot Hueneme"

SENT		ELEVENTH NAVAL DISTRICT		SENT	
DEPT. OR OFFICE ORIGINATING	RELEASE: (TYPE NAME-WRITE INITIALS)		CWO RELEASE	SECURITY CLASSIFICATION	TYPE DESIRED PRECEDENCE. BELOW:
COMELEVEN					PRIORITY, ROUTINE. DEFERRED, MAILGRAM
DATE (LOCAL) 6/9/43		ACTION			ROUTINE

ACTION TO: ACTIVITIES LOS ANGELES AND SAN DIEGO AREA; SANTA BARBARA ADVANCE BASE DEPOT PORT HUENEME

INFORMATION TO: Files

HEADING A DOVE	DATE & TIME OF ORGIN (GCT)	BYTH COUP CAGE FEUD REAR ENTO LORA KUNO MAMO GR222 BT

THE COMMANDANT IS SERIOUSLY CONCERNED OVER THE RECENT DISORDERS WHICH HAVE OCCURRED IN

LOS ANGELES AND ITS VICINITY AND WHICH HAVE ASSUMED SUCH SERIOUS PROPORTIONS AS TO

BE BROADCAST ON THE RADIO AND PUBLISHED IN NEWSPAPERS THROUGHOUT THE U.S. X   THE NAVY

IS A DISCIPLINED ORGANIZATION COMPOSED OF LOYAL AND INTELLIGENT MEN AND PARTAKING IN

ANY ACTIVITIES THAT ARE OF THE NATURE OF MOB VIOLENCE IS A DIRECT REFLECTION ON THE

NAVY ITSELF AND ON THE INDIVIDUAL WHO WEARS THE UNIFORM X   IRRESPECTIVE OF WHAT MAY

HAVE BEEN THE ORIGINAL CAUSE OF THESE DISORDERS, THE ENFORCEMENT OF LAW RESTS IN THE

HANDS OF THE CIVILIAN POLICE AND IS NOT A MATTER WHICH SHOULD BE UNDERTAKEN BY ANY

UNAUTHORIZED GROUPS OF NAVY PERSONNEL X   THE COMMANDANT BELIEVES THAT THE MEN NOW

ENGAGING IN THESE DEMONSTRATIONS ARE ACTUATED MAINLY BY A DESIRE FOR EXCITEMENT AND

FEELS THAT THEY HAVE NOT SERIOUSLY CONSIDERED THE CONSEQUENCES WHICH MAY FOLLOW FROM

ILL CONSIDERED ACTION X   THE COMMANDANT SUGGESTS THAT COMMANDING OFFICERS BRIEF THE

OFFICE	COMDT	INTEL	CIVILIAN PERSONNEL	PLANNING	MATERIEL	NAVAL PERSONNEL	COMM	LEGAL	OPRN	
ACTION										
INFO		X							X	
OFFICE	PORT DIRECTOR	ISSUING	MEDICAL	SUPPLY DEPOT	DISBURSING	DESTROYER STORES	NAVY RELIEF	PUBLIC WORKS	COMMISSARY STORE	
ACTION										
INFO										

PLEASE INITIAL IN APPROPRIATE SPACE ABOVE

DEPT. OR OFFICE ORIGINATING	RELEASE: (TYPE NAME-WRITE INITIALS)	CWO RELEASE	SECURITY CLASSIFICATION	TYPE DESIRED PRECEDENCE. BELOW: PRIORITY, ROUTINE, DEFERRED, MAILGRAM

SENT — ELEVENTH NAVAL DISTRICT — SENT

DATE (LOCAL)

ACTION

ACTION TO:

INFORMATION TO:

HEADING	DATE & TIME OF ORGIN (GCT)	

PAGE TWO (CONTINUED)

SUBSTANCE OF THE ABOVE MEMORANDUM T THE ATTENTION OF THE MEN OF THEIR COMMANDS IN A PERSONAL AND UNOFFICIAL MANNER HAVING FULL CONFIDENCE THAT AN APPEAL TO THE INDIVIDUAL BASED ON COMMON SENSE AND REASONABLENESS WILL INVOKE PROMPT RESPONSE ON THE PART OF THE ENLISTED MEN CONCERNED AND THAT THEY WILL REFRAIN FROM SUCH DISORDERS X

BT 1324

1121

OFFICE	COMDT	INTEL	CIVILIAN PERSONNEL	PLANNING	MATERIEL	NAVAL PERSONNEL	COMM	LEGAL	OPRN	
ACTION										
INFO										
OFFICE	PORT DIRECTOR	ISSUING	MEDICAL	SUPPLY DEPOT	DISBURSING	DESTROYER STORES	NAVY RELIEF	PUBLIC WORKS	COMMISSARY STORE	
ACTION										
INFO										

PLEASE INITIAL IN APPROPRIATE SPACE ABOVE

Appendix C

10 June 1943, Memo from DCGO 11nd Long Beach to All Units Under My Command

GS WIAQ NR5 BM 10 JUNE 43

L A QUAQ 101925 Q5U ZRX GR249

ROUTINE

DCGO 11ND LONG BEACH

FROM:
ACTION: ALL UNITS UNDER MY COMMAND

FOLLOWING FROM COMMANDANT 11TH NAVDIST QUOTE THE COMMANDANT IS
SERIOUSLY CONCERNED OVER THE RECENT DISORDERS WHICH HAVE OCCURED IN LOS
ANGELES AND ITS VICINITY AND WHICH HAVE ASSUMED SUCH SERIOUS PROPORTION
AS TO BE BROADCAST ON THE RADIO AND PUBLISHED IN NEWSPAPERS THROUGHOUT
THE US X THE NAVY IS A -50- DISCIPLINED ORGANIZATION COMPOSED OF LOYAL
AND INTELLIGENT MEN AND PARTAKING IN ANY ACTIVITIES THAT ARE OF THE
NATURE OF MOB VIOLENCE IS A DIRECT REFLECTION ON THE NAVY ITSELF AND
ON THE INDIVIDUAL WHO WEARS THE UNIFORM X IRRESPECTIVE OF WHAT MAY
HAVE BEEN THE ORGINAL CAUSE OF THESE DISORDERS -100- THE ENFORCEMENT
OF THE LAW RESTS IN THE HANDS OF THE CIVILIAN POLICE AND IS NOT A
MATTER WHICH SHOULD BE UNDERTAKEN BY ANY UNAUTHORIZED GROUPS OF NAVY
PERSONNEL X THE COMMANDANT BELIEVES THAT THE MEN NOW ENGAGING IN
THESE DEMONSTRATIONS ARE ACTUATED MAINLY BY A DESIRE FOR EXCITEMENT
AND FEELS -150- THAT THEY HAVE NOT SERIOUSLY CONSIDERED THE CONSEQUENCE
WHICH MAY FOLLOW FROM ILL CONSIDERED ACTION X THE COMMANDANT SUGGESTS
THAT COMMANDING OFFICERS BRING THE SUBSTANCE OF THE ABOVE TO THE ATTEN
ION OF THE MEN OF THEIR COMMANDS IN A PERSONAL AND UNOFFICIAL MANNER
HAVING FULL CONFIDENCE THAT AN APPEAL TO -200- THE INDIVIDUAL BASED
ON COMMON SENSE AND REASONABLENESS WILL INVOKE PROMPT RESPONSE ON THE

FOLLOWING FROM COMMANDANT 11TH NAVDIST QUOTE THE COMMANDANT IS
SERIOUSLY CONCERNED OVER THE RECENT DISORDERS WHICH HAVE OCCURED IN LOS
ANGELES AND ITS VICINITY AND WHICH HAVE ASSUMED SUCH SERIOUS PROPORTION
AS TO BE BROADCAST ON THE RADIO AND PUBLISHED IN NEWSPAPERS THROUGHOUT
THE US X THE NAVY IS A -50- DISCIPLINED ORGANIZATION COMPOSED OF LOYAL
AND INTELLIGENT MEN AND PARTAKING IN ANY ACTIVITIES THAT ARE OF THE
NATURE OF MOB VIOLENCE IS A DIRECT REFLECTION ON THE NAVY ITSELF AND
ON THE INDIVIDUAL WHO WEARS THE UNIFORM X IRRESPECTIVE OF WHAT MAY
HAVE BEEN THE ORGINAL CAUSE OF THESE DISORDERS -100- THE ENFORCEMENT
OF THE LAW RESTS IN THE HANDS OF THE CIVILIAN POLICE AND IS NOT A
MATTER WHICH SHOULD BE UNDERTAKEN BY ANY UNAUTHORIZED GROUPS OF NAVY
PERSONNEL X THE COMMANDANT BELIEVES THAT THE MEN NOW ENGAGING IN
THESE DEMONSTRATIONS ARE ACTUATED MAINLY BY A DESIRE FOR EXCITEMENT
AND FEELS -150- THAT THEY HAVE NOT SERIOUSLY CONSIDERED THE CONSEQUENCE
WHICH MAY FOLLOW FROM ILL CONSIDERED ACTION X THE COMMANDANT SUGGESTS
THAT COMMANDING OFFICERS BRING THE SUBSTANCE OF THE ABOVE TO THE ATTEN
ION OF THE MEN OF THEIR COMMANDS IN A PERSONAL AND UNOFFICIAL MANNER
HAVING FULL CONFIDENCE THAT AN APPEAL TO -200- THE INDIVIDUAL BASED
ON COMMON SENSE AND REASONABLENESS WILL INVOKE PROMPT RESPONSE ON THE
PART OF THE ENLISTED MEN CONCERNED AND THAT THEY WILL REFRAIN
FROM SUCH DESORDERS UNQUOTE EACH COMMANDING OFFICER AND OFFICER IN
CHARGE WILL BRING THIS TO THE ATTENTION OF ALL PERSONNEL UNDER HIS
COMMAND IMMEDIATELY   BT 101925

TOD 2001

THE 104TH GROUP DELETE -- ITS THE
WORD (THE)   CAN U DO   SORI   K

Appendix D

11 June 1943, Memo from Maxwell Murray, Major General, U.S. Army Commanding, to Headquarters Southern California Sector Western Defense Command, Pasadena, California

RESTRICTED

IMMEDIATE ACTION

HEADQUARTERS SOUTHERN CALIFORNIA SECTOR
WESTERN DEFENSE COMMAND
Pasadena, California

June 11, 1943.

TO: Commanders All Units, Southern California Sector.

    1. The recent incidents connected with the socalled "Zoot Suit" riots involved mob action, and incipient rioting, by many soldiers and other service men.

    2. Prompt action to check such action has been taken, and charges are being preferred against those arrested for inciting or actually participating in these riots.

    3. It is obvious that many soldiers are not aware of the serious nature of riot charges. Convictions in a recent serious riot have resulted in sentence to death or long confinement.

    4. It is desired that the attention of all Military personnel be called immediately to the critical dangers of any form of rioting and that incidents which may start as thoughtless group action in comparatively trivial offenses or boisterous conduct are liable to develop into mob riots of the most serious character. Further, mob rioting usually results in injury to persons in no way connected with the initial causes of the disorder. This is true in the case of the recent disorders, which resulted in affront and injury of some completely innocent civilians.

    5. Military personnel of all ranks must understand that no form of mob violence or rioting will be tolerated, and that offenses of this nature will result in immediate and drastic disciplinary action.

Maxwell Murray

MAXWELL MURRAY,
Major General, U.S. Army
Commanding.

IMMEDIATE ACTION

RESTRICTED

Appendix E

10 June 1943, Letter from San Diego City Councilman Charles C. Dail to Rear Admiral David W. Bagley, U.S.N.; 18 June 1943, Letter from Admiral Bagley responding to Councilman Dail

THE CITY OF SAN DIEGO

SAN DIEGO, CALIFORNIA

June 10, 1943

Rear Admiral David W. Bagley, U.S.N.
Commandant
Eleventh Naval District
San Diego, California

Dear Sir:

The critical situation brought to a head in the Los Angeles area as a result of a lawlessness of certain "zoot suit" wearing gangs is the fore-runner of a more serious and widespread condition, and unless exceptional, precautionary methods are undertaken, serious damage to the war effort in civilian-military relations will develop.

The initiative action being taken by soldiers, sailors and marines for the time directed against so-called "zoot suit" wearers is not that alone. It is, speaking for this locality, and has been aimed at civilians in general. There have been numerous instances in San Diego where members of the military forces have insulted and vilified civilians on public streets; and to cite one instance recently: a Consolidated Aircraft Company official, after objecting to the epithets of a marine, pertaining to his civilian status, was attacked and seriously injured and will be unable to return to his duties for some time, as a result of the injuries sustained. Most civilians just "grin and bear it" rather than precipitate an altercation which would be certain if they resisted.

Every civilian, no matter what type of clothes he is wearing, should be safe on the streets, and it is certainly the belief of the writer that the superior officers of service men should vigorously discourage any adverse attitude they may have to civilians, cautioning the personnel that every civilian is not a "draft dodger" and a "slacker," and that a great majority of such civilians in this industrial area are engaged in the building of vital war materials.

The civilian law enforcement officers of this area are capable, ready, willing and able to enforce civilian laws, and any civilian will be dealt with on the basis of the seriousness of his violation. It is the belief of the writer that if steps are taken at this time to correct the derogatory attitude on the part of soldiers, sailors and marines toward civilians, it would go far to relieve the unchecked and developing animosity perpetrated against civilians in general.

Rear Admiral David W. Bagley, U.S.N.
June 10, 1943 -- 2

Please let me assure you that this letter is prompted solely by a strong patriotic desire to help check a situation which certainly is not conducive to cooperative effort on the part of civilien and military forces.

Respectfully yours,

CHARLES C. DAIL,
Councilman,
The City of San Diego

ND11/P8-5
(A3-Wo)

18 June 1943

Mr. Charles C. Dail
Member of the Council
City of San Diego
Civic Center
San Diego, California

Dear Sir:

Receipt is acknowledged of your letter of 10 June 1943 which, it is noted, was published in the local newspapers on the date on which it was received by me, without either my advance knowledge or my concurrence.

As your letter is written on the official stationery of the City of San Diego and signed by you as Councilman, it might appear to be an expression of opinion on the part of the City Council and the Municipality. However, in view of the attending circumstances I assume that it represents your viewpoint as an individual.

I do not condone any such attitude on the part of Naval personnel toward civilians as that reported in your letter. This is a situation definitely to be avoided and the education of service men with regard to their conduct and responsibilities while on liberty is, and always has been, a part of the Naval training system. I might point out that civilian law enforcement agencies are fully empowered to arrest any person of the Naval service guilty of disorderly conduct. Furthermore, appropriate action will be taken on any specific case of misconduct, supported by proper evidence, which is presented to me.

The relations between the personnel of the Navy and the people of the City of San Diego have always been of a most cordial character, and it is my earnest desire that they shall continue.

For purposes of record, I am forwarding a copy of this reply to the Mayor of the City of San Diego.

Very truly yours,

D. W. BAGLEY,
Rear Admiral, U. S. Navy,
Commandant, 11th Naval District.

Ch. of Staff	
Aide	
Accounting and Disb.	
Chaplain	
Comdr's. Clerk	
Communi- cations	
Dist. S.O. OinC. NSD	
Intelligence	
Issuing	
Legal	
Material	
Medical	
Operations	
Personnel (Navy)	
Personnel (Reserve)	
Personnel (Civilian)	
P.D.(NTS)	
Pres.. GCM	
P.W.O.	
Sr. Pat.	
War Plans	
ASSISTANTS Initia Below	

cc: The Mayor.

Appendix F

11 June 1943, Telephone conversation between Captain Heim and Admiral Bagley

TELEPHONE CONVERSATION
BETWEEN ADMIRAL BAGLEY AND CAPTAIN HEIM
AT 1035, JUNE 11, 1943

Captain Heim:
*** they had the Mexican consul and had the press-Mexican and
Spanish press in the area-; they had the Mayor of the City and
Chief of Police and sheriff of the County; they had Congressmen
and government representatives - representatives of everything;
juvenile court people. The meeting was supposed to be off the
record and they wanted a free discussion. The Mexican consul
said it was a juvenile problem of underprivileged second generation foreigners and was backed up by juvenile court people and
Bishop McGregor of the Catholic church who was appointed by
the Governor to head the investigation committee. He agreed
and said it happens to Irishmen, Germans, Czechoslovakians
when the second generation grows up and doesn't get the privileges
and get an inferiority complex. It has grown from things like
not being allowed to go to certain schools, swimming pools,
or to live in certain areas. It has been badly handled by
the the juvenile court.

The concensus of opinion was that there was no subversive
activity, although subversives have taken advantage of the
situation to capitalize on it, but, Admiral, what they are
hurt about the situation - and oh, how they are hurt - is
the City of Los Angeles being placed out of bounds and the
publicity they are getting and they asked me, "Now, Captain
Heim, isn't it possible for you to increase the patrol up
here and handle the situation and not have the City out of
bounds?". My answer was that you never intended to put the
city out of bounds and are only too anxious to let them come
back whenever it is safe for men in uniform to come on liberty
in that area. I think that they have accomplished a great
deal at the meeting. I have seen your despatch to SecNav
and think it is an excellent despatch and covers the situation
entirely.

Admiral Bagley:
Have you any particular recommendation to make on this matter
of changing the restriction?

Captain Heim:
No, sir, I haven't. One thing, Hollywood representatives there
came to me and asked if we could take Hollywood off. They said
they were organized to take care of so many enlisted men and
had the U.S.O., etc. and there was no trouble there and wanted
to be taken out. I said I would take it under consideration
and I have had people investigating and Hollywood is so located
that men would have to go through this restricted area to get
there and Patrol Officer recommends keeping that on. That is
one particular case.

-2-

Captain Heim:	But I have a recommendation - I think that Fogg is overworked and under-manned up there and I think Leovy, District Patrol Officer, ought to get up there and see the situation and he ought to send him assistance if he needs it.
Admiral Bagley:	I will see that he gets it.
Captain Heim:	That would be the only recommendation I have at the present time. As soon as it quiets down if you can release the restriction it would be a good thing.
Admiral Bagley:	Well, yes, that is what I mean to do. In my opinion putting these restrictions on is what has caused them to take measures to stop this. If they think that I am going to release it until it is safe they are wrong.
Captain Heim:	The Army has put certain area out, small one, and play to the public. They didn't back us up as strongly as I would like to see them do it.
Admiral Bagley:	I talked to General Murray and told him what I proposed to do and he agreed it was a good thing but said he would only put on much larger patrol and handle it that way.
Captain Heim:	Of course they have a large military police and have thousands of men scattered in strategic points.
Admiral Bagley:	You say that you have no particular recommendation, take it that you mean you believe it is the best thing to keep the restriction on at least on the weekend.
Captain Heim:	It has been a good thing in two ways - it was good for the city and our men need discipline. We find that there are no old timers but that they are the young reservists just caught and they are egged on by civilians telling them what fine job they are doing and by the press. Yesterday Fogg tells me, just to show you how they get worked up, a draft of men came through the station and read about this in the papers and 8 men got out and left; they were supposed to wait at the station for their train, but they started a band and looked for zoot-suiters and started some trouble. The Patrol round them up and locked them up but it just shows how excited they get about it from just reading the papers.
Admiral Bagley:	Well, Dutch, I am glad to have this first-hand report and I will speak to Leovy about your recommendation in this regard.
Captain Heim:	Fogg is an excellent man but he is overworked and under-staffed. He had a fairly good patrol but had to put them on railroad trains and he has never had his force replenished for that purpose. A group of civilians came to me and said,

-3-

Captain Heim: (Cont'd)	"Don't you think it would be a good idea to increase the patrol just to handle your own men and not civilians?" I said that was being considered all the time.
Admiral Bagley:	They must realize that all men on patrol are taken off vital training and other activities. It isn't like we had an unlimited number of men for the purpose.
Captain Heim:	And a situation like this is of course unexpected and takes priority.

Admiral Bagley:	Of course I don't propose to release this restriction until I am assured that Los Angeles can themselves provide, with their police, the safety of both civilians and visiting Navy people and I shall not follow the recommendation to take off restriction and put on heavier patrol because I want them to do it themselves. Do you agree?
Captain Heim:	Absolutely. I think probably after the weekend it will clear up.
Admiral Bagley:	I think so and hope so and in that event I will be delighted to remove the restriction.
Captain Heim:	I think your despatch about appealing individually to the men is a good thing.
Admiral Bagley:	I got one of those ideas from your letter.
Captain Heim:	I have only one suggestion there. You said in the end, "It is suggested--" I believe it would be better if you ordered every commanding officer to do it.
Admiral Bagley:	I want to discourage this phrase "out of bounds."
Captain Heim:	There is where the press got in. They didn't follow Anderson's notice. I had that read up there yesterday to show you had no intention of placing the city "out of bounds". At the end of the meeting they called on the press for remarks and then I inserted that.
Admiral Bagley:	Yes. Well thank you very much for the report.
Captain Heim:	Yes, sir.
Admiral Bagley:	Is there anything else?
Captain Heim:	No, I haven't.
Admiral Bagley:	I knew you would do a good job.
Captain Heim:	It was most interesting; very intelligent men, very earnest and upset about the whole thing.
Admiral Bagley:	Thank you very much.

Notes

Preface

1. Ilza Veith, *Hysteria, The History of a Disease*.
2. Gustave Le Bon, *The Crowd*.
3. George Rude, *The Crowd in History*, p. 242.
4. Ibid., p. 4.
5. Clifford Geertz, *The Interpretation of Cultures*, part 4.

1. Introduction

1. Peter Shaw, *American Patriots and the Rituals of Revolution*, p. 5.
2. Leonard Pitt, *The Decline of the Californios*, p. 309.
3. Adolfo Ortega, *Caló Tapestry*, p. 38.
4. Jay B. Rosensweig, *Caló*, p. 12.
5. Ortega, *Caló*, pp. 9-10.
6. Carey McWilliams, *North from Mexico*, p. 242.
7. Ibid.
8. Beatrice Griffith, *American Me*, p. 51.
9. McWilliams, *North from Mexico*, p. 230.
10. Griffith, *American Me*, p. 51.
11. Ibid.
12. Carlos Monsiváis, "The Culture of the Frontier," in *Views across the Border*, p. 63.
13. Ibid.
14. Ibid.
15. Joan W. Moore et al., *Homeboys, Gangs, Drugs and Prison in the Barrios of Los Angeles*, p. 70.
16. Ibid., p. 71.
17. Ibid., p. 64.
18. Ibid., p. 65.

19. Alan Jenkins, *The Forties*, p. 103.
20. Ibid.
21. Ibid.
22. Ibid.
23. Geoffrey Perrett, *Days of Sadness, Years of Triumph*, p. 132
24. Ibid.
25. Richard R. Lingeman, *Don't You Know There's a War on?*, p. 333.
26. Fritz Redl, "Zoot-Suits: An Interpretation," p. 259.
27. Ibid.
28. Ibid., p. 260.
29. Ibid.
30. Ibid., p. 259.
31. Erik H. Erikson, *Young Man Luther, a Study in Psychoanalysis and History*, p. 102.
32. Ibid.
33. Peter L. Giovacchini, "Productive Procrastination: Technical Factors in the Treatment of the Adolescent," in *Adolescent Psychiatry*, p. 355.
34. Herbert A. Block and Arthur Niederhoffer, *The Gang, a Study in Adolescent Behavior*, p. 106.
35. Perrett, *Days of Sadness*, p. 245.

2. The Sleepy Lagoon Case

1. Quoted in Jack Smith, "The Great Los Angeles Air Raid," in *Los Angeles, Biography of a City,* p. 364.
2. Ibid., p. 365.
3. Ibid.
4. Ibid., p. 366.
5. Victor Turner, *The Ritual Process*, pp. 131-165.
6. Ibid., p. 203.
7. Carey McWilliams, *North from Mexico*, p. 227.
8. Rodolfo Acuña, *Occupied America, the Chicano's Struggle toward Liberation,* p. 324.
9. McWilliams, *North from Mexico*, pp. 230-231.
10. Jesus Salvador Treviño, "Sleepy Lagoon Revisited, an Interview with Mr. George Shibley" (interviewed on 9 February 1970), on file in the Special Collections of the Chicano Library at the University of California, Los Angeles.

11. Matt S. Meir and Feliciano Rivera, eds., *Readings on La Raza, The Twentieth Century*, p. 128. A complete transcript of the Ayres testimony can be found in Solomon James Jones, "The Government Riots of Los Angeles, June, 1943," pp. 128-136. It can also be found in Grand Jury, Los Angeles County, *Minutes*.
12. Meir and Rivera, *Readings on La Raza,* p. 129.
13. Ibid., p. 130.
14. Ibid.
15. Ibid., p. 131.
16. Ibid., p. 128.
17. Ibid., p. 130.
18. Ibid.
19. Ibid.
20. Guy Endore, *The Sleepy Lagoon Mystery,* p. 18.
21. Ibid.
22. *The Sleepy Lagoon Case*, introduction by Orson Welles, p. 22.
23. Ibid., p. 18.
24. Ibid., p. 19.
25. Ibid., p. 21.
26. Ibid., p. 22.
27. Richard Hofstadter, *The Paranoid Style in American Politics and Other Essays,* p. 4.
28. Sigmund Freud, "Psychoanalytic Notes on an Autobiographical Account of a Case of Paranoia," in *The Standard Edition of the Complete Psychological Works of Sigmund Freud*, pp. 3-82.
29. Hofstadter, *Paranoid Style*, p. 4.
30. Ibid., p. 6.

3. The "Zoot-Suit Yokum" Conspiracy

1. Geoffrey Perrett, *Days of Sadness, Years of Triumph*, p.381.
2. Ibid.
3. John Morton Blum, *V Was for Victory*, p. 37.
4. Ibid.
5. Ibid.
6. Ibid.
7. Richard R. Lingeman, *Don't You Know There's a War on?*, pp.305-306.

8. David Manning White, ed., *From Dogpatch to Slobbovia.* There is no pagination in this book, therefore all subsequent notes will merely be indicated by ibid.

9. Ibid.

10. Arthur Asa Berger, *Li'l Abner, a Study in American Satire*, pp. 77-88.

11. White, *Dogpatch*.

12. Lingeman, *There's a War on*, p. 304.

13. White, *Dogpatch*.

14. Berger, *Li'l Abner*, p. 79.

15. Ibid.

16. Ibid.

17. Ibid.

18. Ibid., p. 91.

19. Ibid.

20. Ibid., p.84.

21. *Los Angeles Times*, 13 June 1943, part 2, p.2.

22. Berger, *Li'l Abner*, p. 85.

23. *Los Angeles Times*, 10 June 1943, Part 1, p. A.

24. Berger, *Li'l Abner*, p. 85.

25. Ibid.

26. Ibid.

27. Ibid.

28. Silvano Arieti, *Creativity, the Magic Synthesis*, pp. 207-208.

29. *Los Angeles Times*, 31 May 1943, part 1, p. 13.

30. Ernst Kris, *Psychoanalytic Explorations in Art*, p. 45.

31. Ibid.

32. Ibid., p. 44.

33. Ibid.

34. Ibid.

4. Servicemen and Zoot-Suiters

1. "Tolerance versus Conformity," in Richard Pollenberg, ed., *America at War: The Home Front, 1941-1945*, p. 91.

2. Ibid.

3. Franco Fornari, *The Psychoanalysis of War*, p. x.

4. Russell F. Weigley, *The American Way of War*, p. 281.

5. John Morton Blum, *V Was for Victory*, p. 57.

6. Ibid.

7. Richard R. Lingeman, *Don't You Know There's a War on?*, p. 302.
8. Blum, *Victory*, p. 53.
9. *Los Angeles Times*, 20 May 1943, part 1, p. 1.
10. *Los Angeles Times*, 16 May 1943, part 1, p. 1.
11. Ibid.
12. Ibid., part 1, p. 15.
13. *Newsweek*, 24 May 1943, p. 15.
14. *Time*, 7 June 1943, pp. 60-61.
15. Ibid.
16. Irving L. Janis, "Psychodynamics of Adjustment to Army Life," p. 162.
17. Ibid.
18. S. Kirkson Weinberg, "Problems of Adjustment in Army Units," p. 276.
19. Ibid.
20. Janis, "Psychodynamics," p. 163.
21. Ibid.
22. Ibid., pp. 163-164.
23. Anna Freud, *The Writings of Anna Freud*, p. 113.
24. Weinberg, "Adjustment in Army Units," p. 277.
25. James Jones, *WWII*, p. 3.
26. Ibid.
27. I determined this number through a perusal of the *Los Angeles Times* reports on civilian-servicemen violence in the greater Los Angeles-San Diego areas for the period of 15-30 May 1953. See chapter 5, note 3 for a precise breakdown of each case.
28. *Los Angeles Times*, 18 May 1943, part 3, p. 3.
29. See Abraham Hoffman, *Unwanted Mexican Americans in the Great Depression—Repatriation Pressures, 1929-1939.*
30. Bill Hosokawa, *Nisei*, p. 269.
31. Lingeman, *There's a War on*, p. 87.
32. Ibid.
33. Ibid., pp. 87-88.
34. Joan W. Moore et al., *Homeboys, Gangs, Drugs and Prison in the Barrios of Los Angeles*, p. 64.
35. Geoffrey Perrett, *Days of Sadness, Years of Triumph*, p. 349.
36. Ibid.
37. Ibid., p. 350.

38. Ibid., p. 349.
39. Solomon James Jones, "The Government Riots of Los Angeles, June, 1943," pp. 141-142.
40. Ibid., p. 142.
41. Beatrice Griffith, *American Me*, p. 75.
42. Ibid., p. 73.
43. Kai Erikson, *Wayward Puritans, a Study in the Sociology of Deviance*, p. 28.
44. Marilyn Domer, "The Zoot-Suit Riot: A Culmination of Social Tensions in Los Angeles," p. 68.
45. Patricia Rae Adler, "The 1943 Zoot-Suit Riot: Brief Episode in a Long Conflict," in *An Awakening Minority: The Mexican-Americans*, p. 152.
46. Ibid.
47. Chester B. Himes, *"Zoot Riots Are Race Riots,"* p. 200.
48. Ibid.
49. See Raúl Morín, *Among the Valiant*.
50. Ibid., p. 87.
51. Ibid.
52. Meyer H. Maskin and Leon L Altman, "Military Psychodynamics, Psychological Factors in the Transition from Civilian to Soldier," p. 268.
53. Carey McWilliams, *North from Mexico*, p. 240.
54. Rodolfo Acuña, *Occupied America, the Chicano's Struggle toward Liberation*, pp. 169-170.

5. The Zoot-Suit Riots

1. Henry Elkin, "Aggressive and Erotic Tendencies in Army Life," p. 409.
2. *Los Angeles Times*, 16 May 1943, part 1, p. 15.
3. *Los Angeles Times*, 15 May 1943, part 1, p. 6, 21 May 1943, p. A, 25 May 1943, part 1, p. 10, 25 May 1943, part 2, p. 2, 29 May 1943, p. A, 30 May 1943, part 2, p. 2.
4. *Los Angeles Times*, 18 May 1943, part 2, p. 3.
5. *Los Angeles Times*, 4 June 1943, part 1, p. 10. The headline indicated there had been a stabbing; however, the one stabbed was a young non-zoot-suit-wearing Mexican American.
6. Carey McWilliams, *North from Mexico*, p. 245.
7. Ibid.

8. Ibid.
9. Ibid.
10. Ibid.
11. Beatrice Griffith, *American Me*, p. 20.
12. Ibid.
13. Ibid., p. 19.
14. Ibid., p. 20.
15. Letter from Councilman Charles C. Dail to Admiral David W. Bagley, Commandant Eleventh Naval District, 10 June 1943, Federal Archives and Records Center, Laguna Niguel, California, File P8-5.
16. Ibid.
17. McWilliams, *North from Mexico*, p. 250.
18. Dale Drum, "Report Prepared at the Los Angeles Navy Recruiting Station and Office of Naval Procurement," 18 May 1951, p. 5. Photo copy from Special Collections of the Chicano Library, University of California, Los Angeles.
19. Ibid., p. 6.
20. Ibid., p. 7.
21. Ibid.
22. *Los Angeles Times*, 9 June 1943, part 2, p. 1.
23. "Activities Los Angeles and San Diego Area, Santa Barbara Advance Base Depot Port Hueneme," Federal Archives and Records Center, Laguna Niguel, California, File P8-5.
24. Ibid.
25. Sigmund Freud, "Group Psychology and the Analysis of the Ego," in *The Standard Edition of the Complete Psychological Works of Sigmund Freud*, p. 95.
26. Griffith, *American Me*, pp. 21-22.
27. "Activities Los Angeles and San Diego Area," n.p.
28. Ibid.
29. "Telephone Conversation between Admiral Bagley and Captain Heim at 1035, June 11, 1943," Federal Archives and Records Center, Laguna Niguel, California, File P8-5.
30. Memo, "0045, June 8, 1943," Federal Archives and Records Center, Laguna Niguel, California, File P8-5.
31. Ibid.
32. "Telephone Conversation," p. 2.
33. Ibid.
34. Marilyn Domer, "The Zoot-Suit Riot: A Culmination of

Social Tensions in Los Angeles," p. 89.

35. Ibid.
36. Memo, "0045, June 8, 1943," n.p.
37. Domer, "Zoot-Suit Riot," p. 87.
38. McWilliams, *North from Mexico*, p. 248.
39. Griffith, *American Me*, p. 24.
40. Ibid.
41. Ibid.
42. Office of the City Clerk, City of Los Angeles, Council File 15079, Resolution introduced by Councilman Norris J. Nelson, 9 June 1943.
43. Griffith, *American Me*, p. 23.
44. Ibid., p. 26.
45. Ibid.
46. Report of the Joint Fact-Finding Committee on Un-American Activities in California, 1943, p. 164.
47. Ibid.
48. Ibid., p. 171.
49. Ibid., p. 161.
50. Marion Bachrach, "The Truth about Los Angeles," p. 12.
51. Ibid.
52. Ibid., p. 13.
53. Ibid.
54. Telegram from Alfredo Elías, Consul of Mexico, to Admiral David W. Bagley, 9 June 1943, Federal Archives and Records Center, Laguna Niguel, California, File P8-5.
55. "Telephone Conversation," p. 1.
56. Ibid.

6. The Symbols, Imagery, and Rhetoric of the Riots

1. See Thurgood Marshall, "Gestapo in Detroit," pp. 232-233, 246-247; Robert Shogan and Tom Craig, *The Detroit Race Riot: A Study in Violence*; Harvard Sitkoff, "The Detroit Race Riot of 1943," pp. 183-194.
2. *Los Angeles Daily News* (hereafter cited as *Daily News*), 8 June 1943, p. 3.
3. Carey McWilliams, *North from Mexico,* p. 245.
4. The term "convoy" was first used by the *Los Angeles Examiner* (hereafter cited as *Examiner*) on 5 June 1943, p. 3; the

Los Angeles Herald-Express (hereafter cited as *Herald-Express*) chose to use the term "task-force" in describing the activities of the servicemen on 5 June 1943 (p. 1).

5. *Examiner*, 6 June 1943, part 2, p. 1.
6. Ibid.
7. *Herald-Express*, 9 June 1943, p. 6.
8. *Daily News*, 11 June 1943, p. 1.
9. *Los Angeles Times*, 10 June 1943, part 1, p. 1.
10. Ibid., 8 June 1943, part 1, p. 1.
11. The hysteria over Mexican intervention during World War I on the side of the Entente powers was precipitated by a secret telegram sent to Mexico via the German ambassador to the United States in Washington. The telegram, drafted by German foreign secretary Arthur Zimmermann, suggested that Mexico participate in an offensive alliance against the United States, further suggesting that Germany would guarantee the return of the territories lost during the Mexican-American War. The telegram was intercepted and decoded by British admiralty intelligence, who in turn made it available to President Woodrow Wilson. For a popular history, see Barbara Tuchman, *The Zimmermann Telegram*.
12. *Daily News,* 9 June 1943, p. 1.
13. Ibid., 8 June 1943, p. 6.
14. *Examiner,* 11 June 1943, part 2, p. 12.
15. *Los Angeles Times*, 5 June 1943, part 1, p. 1.
16. *Daily News,* 8 June 1943, p. 3.
17. Ibid., 7 June 1943, p. 1.
18. Ibid.
19. Marilyn Domer, "The Zoot-Suit Riot: A Culmination of Social Tensions in Los Angeles," p. 119.
20. Ibid., p. 89.
21. Ibid.
22. *Report of the Joint Fact-Finding Committee on Un-American Activities in California*, 1943, p. 161.
23. Ibid.
24. Domer, "Zoot-Suit Riot," pp. 86-87.
25. Ibid., p. 69.
26. Ibid., p. 101.
27. Chester B. Himes, "Zoot Riots Are Race Riots," pp. 200-201, 222.

28. *Time*, 21 June 1943, p. 18.
29. Lloyd Mallan, "Axis Propaganda in Latin America," p. 37.
30. Leonard Pitt, *The Decline of the Californios* , p. 293.
31. "American Embassy, Office of the Naval Attaché, Mexico City, Mexico," 4 June 1943, Federal Archives and Records Center, Laguna Niguel, California, File E-744.
32. Ibid.
33. Ibid.
34. "Reaction of Mexican Naval Vessels' Crews to Treatment Received in U.S.," Federal Archives and Records Center, Laguna Niguel, California, File E-744.
35. "American Embassy," n.p.
36. Los Angeles County Grand Jury, "Report of the Special Committee on Racial Problems," p. 27.
37. Quoted in Domer, "Zoot-Suit Riot," p. 105.
38. Ibid., p. 108; Beatrice Griffith, *American Me*, p. 26.
39. Arturo Madrid-Barela, "In Search of the Authentic Pachuco: An Interprative Essay," pp. 34-35.
40. Domer, "Zoot-Suit Riot," p. 120.
41. Griffith, *American Me*, p. 48.
42. Domer, Zoot-Suit Riot," pp. 89-90.
43. Ibid., p. 90.
44. *Los Angeles Times*, 8 June 1943, part 1, p. A.
45. Joan W. Moore et al., *Homeboys, Gangs, Drugs and Prison in the Barrios of Los Angeles*, p. 59.
46. *Los Angeles Times*, 11 June 1943, part 1, p. A.
47. Irving L. Janis, "Psychodynamics of Adjustment to Army Life," p. 172.
48. Henry Elkin, "Aggressive and Erotic Tendencies in Army Life," p. 409.
49. Peter Bourne, "Some Observations on the Psychosocial Phenomena Seen in Basic Training,", p. 189.
50. Ibid.
51. Ibid.
52. Ibid.
53. Here I refer to the concept of degradation ceremonies as presented by Harold Garfinkel in "Conditions of Successful Degradation Ceremonies."
54. Erik J. Hobsbawn, *Primitive Rebels,* p. 150.
55. Geoffrey Perrett, *Days of Sadness, Years of Triumph,* p. 233.

56. Ibid.
57. Edwin S. Schneidman and Norman L. Farberow, *Clues to Suicide*, p. 73.
58. See chapter 7.
59. Robert Jay Lifton, *Death in Life*, pp. 500-506.
60. Eric J. Leed, *No Man's Land*, p. 27.
61. Richard Pollenberg, *War and Society*, p. 137.
62. James Jones, *WWII*, p. 150.
63. Ibid.
64. Letter from Councilman Charles C. Dail to Admiral David W. Bagley, Commandant Eleventh Naval District, 10 June 1943, Federal Archives and Records Center, Laguna Niguel, California, File P8-5.
65. Mircea Eliade, *The Sacred and the Profane*, p. 208.
66. Ibid., p. 208.
67. Arnold van Gennap, *The Rites of Passage*, p. 94.
68. Victor W. Turner, *The Ritual Process*, p. 94.
69. Leed, *No Man's Land*, p. 17.
70. Ibid., p. 24.
71. Turner, *Ritual Process*, p. 95.
72. Richard R. Lingeman, *Don't You Know There's a War on?*, p. 334.
73. Turner, *Ritual Process*, p. 167.
74. Ibid., p. 176.
75. Natalie Zeomn Davis, "Women on Top: Symbolic Sexual Inversion and Political Disorder in Early Modern Europe," in *The Reversible World*, p. 153.
76. Ibid.
77. Raúl Morín, *Among the Valiant*, p. 56.

7. "The Hard to Get At"

1. Memo, "The Senior Patrol Officer to *Comeleven*," 29 July 1943, Federal Archives and Records Center, Laguna Niguel, California, File P-8.
2. Ibid., p. 2.
3. Ibid.
4. Ibid.
5. Ibid.
6. Ibid.

7. Ibid.
8. "Organized Personnel Available for Riot Duty on Terminal Island," Restricted, 29 July 1943, Federal Archives and Records Center, Laguna Niguel, California, File NB-66, MN/p16-1.
9. Memo, "The Senior Patrol Officer to Comeleven," 16 October 1943, Federal Archives and Records Center, Laguna Niguel, California, File QL/P13-4.
10. Ibid.
11. Ibid.
12. *Report of the Joint Fact-Finding Committee on Un-American Activities in California*, 1945, p. 174.
13. Ibid., p. 182.
14. Ibid., p. 181.
15. Ibid.
16. Ibid.
17. Ibid., p. 160.
18. Ibid., pp. 173-174.
19. Carey McWilliams, *North from Mexico*, p. 255.
20. Ibid.
21. Beatrice Griffith, *American Me*, p. 27.
22. Ibid.
23. Albert Deutsch, *Our Rejected Children*, p. 115.
24. California Youth Authority, *Report of Program and Progress, 1943-1948*, p. 91.
25. Ibid.
26. Ibid.
27. Ibid.
28. Ibid., p. 94.
29. Ibid.
30. Deutsch, *Rejected Children*, p. 115.
31. California Youth Authority, *Progress*, p. 106.
32. Duane Robinson, *Chance to Belong*, p. 2.
33. Ibid.
34. Ibid., p. 9.
35. California Youth Authority, *Progress*, p. 16.
36. Robinson, *Chance to Belong*, p. 115.
37. Ibid.
38. Ibid.

39. Ibid., p. 20.
40. Joan W. Moore et al., *Homeboys, Gangs, Drugs and Prison in the Barrios of Los Angeles*, p. 84.
41. Ibid.
42. Ibid., p. 85.
43. For a statement on the goals of the journal see Karl Holton, "Youth Authority Quarterly," p. 3.
44. Harry Isbell, "Meeting a Growing Menace—Drug Addiction," pp. 29-36.
45. Lorenzo S. Buckley, "The Naline Program."
46. "Racial Conditions (Spanish-Mexican Activities) Los Angeles Field Division, " Federal Bureau of Investigation, Los Angeles, California, 14 January 1944, no file number.
47. Ibid., p. 53.
48. Ibid., p. 4.
49. Ibid.
50. Ibid., p. 13.
51. Ibid.
52. Ibid.
53. Ibid.
54. Ibid., p. 54.
55. Ibid., p. 6.
56. Ibid., p. 43.
57. Ibid., p. 44.
58. Ibid.
59. Ibid.
60. Ibid., p. 51. The FBI reference is from Emory Bogardus, "Gangs of Mexican-American Youths," pp. 55-66.
61. Federal Bureau of Investigation report of 12 March 1945, p. 2, no file number.
62. Ibid.
63. Federal Bureau of Investigation report of 14 January 1944, p. 54, no file number.
64. For a study of the private organizations that investigated zoot-suiters, see Ismael Dieppa, "The Zoot-Suit Riots Revisited: The Role of Private Philanthropy in Youth Problems of Mexican-Americans."
65. Ruth Tuck, *Not with the Fist*, pp. vii-viii.

8. Between Annihilation and Redemption

1. Dorothy Bloch, "Feelings that Kill: The Effect of the Wish for Infanticide in Neurotic Depression," p. 51.
2. Franco Fornari, *The Psychoanalysis of War*, p. 13. Although rarely used in psychoanalytic literature, Fornari introduces the theme of infanticide by referring to the "Cronus complex," which he explains in these terms: "This is the inverse of the Oedipus complex. It consists primarily in the father's unconscious hostility and rivalry in relation to his sons, and in his unconscious wish to castrate, humiliate, and annihilate them. In the Greek myth, Cronus devours his sons"(p. 12, note 3). Also see Edward Glover, *War, Sadism, and Pacifism*.
3. Fornari, *Psychoanalysis of War*, p. 7.
4. Ibid.
5. John Knowles, *A Separate Peace*, p. 193.
6. Geoffrey Perrett, *Days of Sadness, Years of Triumph*, p. 339.
7. Robert Jay Lifton, *The Broken Connection*, pp. 302-303.
8. Erik H. Erikson, *Childhood and Society*, pp. 307-308.
9. Octavio Paz, *The Labyrinth of Solitude*, pp. 13-14.
10. Ibid., p. 14.
11. Ibid.
12. Ibid., p. 13
13. Samuel Ramos, *Profile of Man and Culture in Mexico*, p. 56.
14. Ibid., p. 58.
15. Ibid., p. 57, footnote 2.
16. Ibid., pp. 58-59.
17. Ibid., p. 61.
18. Ibid., p. 59.
19. Paz, *Labyrinth*, p. 17.
20. Ibid.
21. Manuel P. Servín, "The Post-World War II Mexican-American, 1925-1965: A Nonachieving Minority," in *An Awakening Minority: The Mexican-Americans*, p. 168.
22. Carey McWilliams, *North from Mexico*, p. 241.
23. Ibid.
24. Ibid.
25. Ibid., p. 249.
26. Moses Rischin, "Continuities and Discontinuities in Spanish-Speaking California, " in *Ethnic Conflict in California*

History, p. 48.

27. Octavio Romano, "The Historical and Intellectual Presence of Mexican-Americans," pp. 39-40.
28. Luis Valdéz, "Once Again, Meet the Zoot-Suiters," *Los Angeles Times*, 13 August 1978, part 5, p. 3.
29. Thomas Sánchez, *Zoot-Suit Murders*.

Bibliography

Acuña, Rodolfo. *Occupied America, the Chicano's Struggle toward Liberation.* New York, 1972, 1981.

Adler, Patricia Rae. "The 1943 Zoot-Suit Riot: Brief Episode in a Long Conflict." In *An Awakening Minority: The Mexican-Americans.* Edited by Manuel P. Servín. Beverly Hills, Calif., 1974.

Arieti, Silvano. *Creativity, the Magic Synthesis.* New York, 1976.

Bachrach, Marion. "The Truth about Los Angeles." *New Masses*, 6 July 1943.

Baechler, Jean. *Suicides.* 1979.

Bakan, David. *Slaughter of the Innocents.* San Francisco, Calif., 1971.

Berger, Arthur Asa. *Li'l Abner, a Study in American Satire.* New York, 1970.

Berger, Peter, et al. *The Homeless Mind, Modernization and Consciousness.* New York, 1973.

Bloch, Dorothy. "Fantasy and the Fear of Infanticide." *Psychoanalytic Review* 61, no. 1 (Spring 1974).

――――. "Feelings that Kill: The Effect of the Wish for Infanticide in Neurotic Depression." *Psychoanalytic Review* 52, no. 1 (Spring 1965).

Block, Herbert A., and Arthur Niederhoffer. *The Gang, a Study in Adolescent Behavior.* New York, 1958.

Blum, John Morton. *V Was for Victory.* New York, 1976.

Bogardus, Emory. "Gangs of Mexican-American Youth." *Sociology and Social Research* 23 (September-October 1943).

Bourne, Peter. "Some Observations on the Psychosocial Phenomena Seen in Basic Training." *Psychiatry* 30, no. 2.

Bouthoul, Gaston. *Les Guerres: Elements de Polemologie.* 1951.

Brissaud, Y. B. "L'Infanticide à la fin du moyen âge, ses motivations psychologiques et sa répression." *Revue de droit français et anger* 50 (1972).

Buckley, Lorenzo S. "The Naline Program." *California Youth Authority Quarterly* 10, no. 2 (Summer 1957).

California Youth Authority. *Report of Program and Progress, 1943-1948*. Sacramento, 1948.

Davis, Natalie Zeomn. "Women on Top: Symbolic Sexual Inversion and Political Disorder in Early Modern Europe." In *The Reversible World*. Edited by Barbara B. Babcock. Ithaca, N.Y., 1978.

de Mause, Lloyd. "The Evolution of Childhood." In *The History of Childhood*. Edited by Lloyd de Mause. New York, 1974.

Deutsch, Albert. *Our Rejected Children*. Boston, 1950.

Dieppa, Ismael. "The Zoot-Suit Riots Revisited: The Role of Private Philanthropy in Youth Problems of Mexican-Americans." Doctoral dissertation, University of Southern California, 1973.

Domer, Marilyn. "The Zoot-Suit Riot: A Culmination of Social Tensions in Los Angeles." Master's thesis, Claremont Graduate School, 1955.

Eliade, Mircea. *The Sacred and the Profane*. New York, 1959.

Elkin, Henry. "Aggressive and Erotic Tendencies in Army Life." *American Journal of Sociology* 51, no. 5 (March 1946).

Endore, Guy. *The Sleepy Lagoon Mystery*. Los Angeles, 1944.

Erikson, Erik H. *Childhood and Society*. New York, 1963.
———. *Young Man Luther, a Study in Psychoanalysis and History*. New York, 1960.

Erikson, Kai. *Wayward Puritans, a Study in the Sociology of Deviance*. New York, 1966.

Fornari, Franco. *The Psychoanalysis of War*. Garden City, N.Y., 1974.

Freud, Anna. *The Writings of Anna Freud*. Volume 2 (1936) of *The Ego and the Mechanisms of Defense*. New York, 1973.

Freud, Sigmund. "Group Psychology and the Analysis of the Ego" (1921). In volume 18 of *The Standard Edition of the Complete Psychological Works of Sigmund Freud*. Edited and translated by James Strachey et al. London, 1953-1956.

_____. "Psychoanalytic Notes on an Autobiographical Account of a Case of Paranoia" (1911). In volume 12 of *The Standard Edition of the Complete Psychological Works of Sigmund Freud.* Edited and translated by James Strachey et al. London, 1953-1956.

Garfinkel, Harold. "Conditions of Successful Degradation Ceremonies." *American Journal of Sociology* 61 (March 1976).

Geertz, Clifford. *The Interpretation of Cultures.* New York, 1973.

Giovacchini, Peter L. "Productive Procrastination: Technical Factors in the Treatment of the Adolescent." In *Adolescent Psychiatry*, volume 4. Edited by Sherman Feinstein and Peter L. Giovacchini. New York, 1973.

Glover, Edward. *War, Sadism, and Pacifism.* London, 1946.

Griffith, Beatrice. *American Me.* Cambridge, Mass., 1948.

Himes, Chester B. "Zoot Riots Are Race Riots." *Crises* 50, no. 7 (July 1943).

Hobsbawn, Eric J. *Primitive Rebels.* New York, 1959.

Hoffman, Abraham. *Unwanted Mexican Americans in the Great Depression—Repatriation Pressures, 1929-1939.* Tucson, 1977.

Hofstadter, Richard. *The Paranoid Style in American Politics and Other Essays.* New York, 1967.

Holton, Karl. "Youth Authority Quarterly." *California Youth Authority Quarterly* 1, no.1 (Summer 1948).

Hosokawa, Bill. *Nisei.* New York, 1969.

Isabell, Harry. "Meeting a Growing Menace—Drug Addiction." *California Youth Authority Quarterly* 5, no. 1 (Spring 1952).

Janis, Irving L. "Psychodynamics of Adjustment to Army Life." *Psychiatry* 8, no. 2 (May 1945).

Jenkins, Alan. *The Forties.* New York, 1977.

Jones, James. *WWII.* New York, 1975.

Jones, Solomon James. "The Government Riots of Los Angeles, June, 1943." Master's thesis, University of California, Los Angeles, 1969.

Knowles, John. *A Separate Peace.* New York,1972.

Kris, Ernst. *Psychoanalytic Explorations in Art.* New York, 1971.

Langer, William. "Infanticide: A Historical Survey." *History of Childhood Quarterly* 2 (1974).

Le Bon, Gustave. *The Crowd.*

Leed, Eric J. *No Man's Land.* Cambridge, England, 1979.

Lifton, Robert Jay. *The Broken Connection.* New York, 1979.
_____ .*Death in Life.* New York, 1969.

Lingeman, Richard R. *Don't You Know There's a War on?* New York, 1976.

Loewenberg, Peter. "The Psychohistorical Origins of the Nazi Youth Cohort." *American Historical Review* 76, no. 5 (December 1971).

Los Angeles County Grand Jury. *Minutes,* 1942.

_____. "Report of the Special Committee on Racial Problems." In *Final Report of the 1943 Los Angeles County Grand Jury.*

Madrid-Barela, Arturo. "In Search of the Authentic Pachuco: An Interpretative Essay." *Aztlán, Chicano Journal of the Social Sciences and the Arts* 4, no. 1 (Spring 1973).

Mallan, Lloyd. "Axis Propaganda in Latin America." *Current History* 5, no. 25 (September 1943).

Marshall, Thurgood. "Gestapo in Detroit." *Crises* 50, no. 8 (August 1943).

Maskin, Meyer H., and Leon L. Altman. "Military Psycho-dynamics, Psychological Factors in the Transition from Civilian to Soldier." *Psychiatry* 6, no. 3 (August 1943).

McWilliams, Carey. *North from Mexico.* Philadelphia, 1949; New York, 1948, 1975.

Meir, Matt S., and Feliciano Rivera, editors. *Readings on La Raza, The Twentieth Century.* New York, 1974.

Monsiváis, Carlos. "The Culture of the Frontier." In *Views across the Border.* Edited by Stanley Ross. Albuquerque, 1978.

Moore, Joan W., et al. *Homeboys, Gangs, Drugs and Prison in the Barrios of Los Angeles.* Philadelphia, 1978.

Morín, Raúl. *Among the Valiant.* Alhambra, Calif., 1966.

Ortega, Adolfo. *Caló Tapestry.* Berkeley, Calif., 1977.

Paz, Octavio. *The Labyrinth of Solitude.* New York, 1961.

Perrett, Geoffrey. *Days of Sadness, Years of Triumph.* Baltimore, 1974.

Pitt, Leonard. *The Decline of the Californios.* Los Angeles, 1971.

Pollenberg, Richard, editor. *America at War: The Home Front,* *1941-1945.* Englewood Cliffs, N.J., 1968.
_____. *War and Society.* Philadelphia, 1972.

Ramos, Samuel. *Profile of Man and Culture in Mexico.* 2d ed. Austin, 1962.

Redl, Fritz. "Zoot-Suits: An Interpretation." *Survey Monthly* 79, no. 10 (October 1943).

Report of the Joint Fact-Finding Committee on Un-American Activities in California. Sacramento, Calif., 1943 and 1945.

Rheingold, Joseph. *The Fear of Being a Woman: A Theory of Maternal Destructiveness.* New York, 1964.

Rischin, Moses. "Continuities and Discontinuities in Spanish-Speaking California." In *Ethnic Conflict in California History.* Edited by Charles Wollenberg. Los Angeles, 1970.

Robinson, Duane. *Chance to Belong.* New York, 1949.

Romano, Octavio. "The Historical and Intellectual Presence of Mexican-Americans." *El Grito* (Winter 1969).

Rosensweig, Jay B. *Caló.* New York, 1973.

Rude, George. *The Crowd in History.* New York.

Sánchez, Thomas. *Zoot-Suit Murders.* New York, 1978.

Schneidman, Edwin S., and Norman L. Farberow. *Clues to Suicide.* New York, 1957.

Servín, Manuel P. "The Post-World War II Mexican-American, 1925-1965: A Nonachieving Minority." In *An Awakening Minority: The Mexican-Americans.* Edited by Manuel P. Servín. Beverly Hills, Calif., 1974.

Shaw, Peter. *American Patriots and the Rituals of Revolution.* Cambridge, England, 1981.

Shogan, Robert, and Tom Craig. *The Detroit Race Riot: A Study in Violence.* Philadelphia, 1964.

Sitkoff, Harvard. "The Detroit Race Riot of 1943." *Michigan History* 53 (Fall 1969).

The Sleepy Lagoon Case. Introduction by Orson Welles. Los Angeles, 1944.

Smith, Jack. "The Great Los Angeles Air Raid." In *Los Angeles, Biography of a City.* Edited by John and La Rue Caughey.

Los Angeles, 1976.

Tuchmann, Barbara. *The Zimmermann Telegram.* New York, 1958.

Tuck, Ruth. *Not with the Fist.* New York, 1946.

Turner, Victor W. *The Ritual Process.* Chicago, 1969.

Valdéz, Luis. "Once Again, Meet the Zoot-Suiters." *Los Angeles Times*, 13 August 1978, part 5, p. 3.

Van Gennap, Arnold. *The Rites of Passage.* Chicago, 1960.

Veith, Ilza. *Hysteria, the History of a Disease.* Chicago, 1970.

Weigley, Russell F. *The American Way of War.* London, 1973.

Weinberg, S. Kirson. "Problems of Adjustment in Army Units." *American Journal of Sociology* 50, no. 4 (January 1945).

White, David Manning, editor. *From Dogpatch to Slobbovia.* Boston, 1964.

Index